AWAKEN YOUR COURSE CREATION MOJO

BEAT PROCRASTINATION AND FIRE UP YOUR COURSE CREATION MOTIVATION

By Sarah Cordiner

Copyright Sarah Cordiner 2017
ISBN-10: 0-9876267-1-X
ISBN-13: 978-0-9876267-1-4

Get Sarah's FREE webinar: *How To Plan Your First Online Course*: www.sarahcordiner.com/PlanYourCourse

Join the Facebook group 'Entrepreneur to Edupreneur'

See the back page of this book for your FREE ECOURSE

Author: Sarah Cordiner
Title: Awaken Your Course Creation Mojo
Subtitle: Beat Procrastination and Fire Up Your Course Creation Motivation
Subjects: Education; Adult Education; Learning Theory and Practice; Curriculum Design and Development, Business, Entrepreneurship, Marketing

Disclaimer: The material in this publication is of the nature of general comment only, and does not represent professional advice. It is not intended to provide specific guidance for particular circumstances, and it should not be relied upon as the basis for any decision to take action or not take action on any matter which it covers. Readers should obtain professional advice where appropriate, before making any such decision. To the maximum extent permitted by law, the author and publisher disclaim all responsibility and liability to any person, arising directly or indirectly from any person taking action or not taking action based on the information in this publication. The moral rights of the author have been asserted.

Acknowledgements

This book goes out to my entire community, particularly the members of my Facebook group 'Entrepreneur to Edupreneur - Course Creators', as many of the members contributed to a survey that I conducted in there to find out what the most common course creation motivational challenges are in order for me to address the biggest ones in this book.

Table of Contents

I Don't Have the Right Idea Yet! 11
Overcome Self-Doubt and The Inner Imposter 19
Overcoming Imposter Syndrome 29
Healthy Fear, Or Out of Alignment? 43
What To Do If The Worst Happens 45
But My Family, Friends & Dog Say I shouldn't Do It 53
Dealing With Your 'Non-Supporters' 59
I've Got More Planning & Research To Do First.................. 67
I'm Not Clear On Why I'm Doing This 81
I Can't Afford To Do It 87
I Don't Have Enough Time 97
What If Nobody Buys It? 103
What if People Steal or Copy my Ideas or IP? 109
What If My Video's Are Not 'Hollywood' Perfect? 125
What If People Criticise Me or Don't Like Me? 129
What If There Is Too Much Competition & I Can't Compete? 157
What If They Think I'm Boring? 185
What If I Have Too Much Content? 187
I'm Overwhelmed By How Much There Is To Do 191
I'm Too Old or Too Young to Teach 197
Time To Create Your Online Course! 201
Connect With Sarah 203

AWAKEN YOUR COURSE CREATION MOJO!

The mojo.

That 'magic thing' that puts us into productivity hyperdrive and has us feeling 'on fire' when it's around, yet we miss like a vital bodily organ if it's not working.

- FEAR
- LACK OF MOTIVATION
- LACK OF KNOWLEDGE
- LOW CONFIDENCE
- LACK OF SUPPORT
- LACK OF EXPERIENCE
- LACK OF FOCUS
- EXCUSES

There are endless causes behind an underperforming course creation mojo, but when it's gone, getting it back is our top priority.

There are many reasons why so many course creators out there haven't started sharing their expertise with the world - or keep retreating back into obscurity each time they peep their toe over the starting line.

It breaks my heart when I think of all of the unfinished courses in the world, all because our inner course creation mojos have taken a hall pass.

In this book I will explore some of the most common course creation mojo-killers and use this opportunity to remind you of your inner brilliance, tell you (nicely) to quit procrastinating, and for the real tough ones, just slap you with a metaphorical wet fish whilst begging you to stop being so selfish for keeping all your knowledge locked away from the world inside that sensational brain of yours (meany).

This book was originally a chapter (and still is) from my book *'Entrepreneur to Edupreneur: The 10 Stages To Creating A Wildly Successful Education-Based Business & Online Course'*, but as I started writing it to answer specific concerns that had been raised by members of my Facebook group (Entrepreneur to Edupreneur), I realised that this had swiftly become a book in it's own right.

I never intended for this topic to be so comprehensive when I first sat down to write the original book. But I have found in my work with edupreneurs that the actual course creation process itself is often not the biggest barrier to people getting their courses out to the world.

The biggest barriers of all are what I call the *'course creation mojo killers'*. And so, it became more than just a chapter of a book and deserved it's own title altogether.

Many of us may be hiding behind the excuses of *'I've not had time to learn how to use my LMS yet'* or *'I'm just waiting for my camera gear to arrive'*, or indeed one of the gazillion excuses I hear everyday and have even used myself!

The reason I use the word excuse, is because it can sometimes be hard to pinpoint exactly what's causing our blockage when our mojo heads off for a sabbatical - but usually the thing we think is our course creation blocker is far from the real cause and why therefore so many edupreneurs get stuck in a never-ending cycle of procrastination and motionless frustration.

If your mojo is missing, let me coax him back for you....

In this book I have outlined the top 17 course creation blockers that I see in the industry every day and provided my perspectives, tips and suggestions for battling through them and bring back that mojo again!

CHAPTER 1

I Don't Have the Right Idea Yet!

Every day I hear people say to me things like *'I'm not creating any courses yet because I'm just waiting until I figure out what my topic should be'*; or *'I'm going to wait until the right idea comes to me'*.

It's as if they think that one day this magical epiphany is just going to bestow upon them and they will know precisely what they are going to do and how to do it.

This breaks my heart; because epiphanies are lies.

It's like people look around them and think that everybody else just fell out of the womb knowing exactly what they were going to do with their lives. Like every successful business just started exactly the way it is the day that it launched.

It can be easy to feel like 'everyone else has got their stuff together', but the truth is, even those with absolutely explicit plans have to step forward with uncertainty and improvisation, as we cannot predict the future. Businesses, ideas, campaigns, products, services, people, the market and everything we have today, could be different tomorrow.

We live in a world of constant change and if what we offer does not change with it, we'll be hanging out with with the Fail-saurus-rex pretty quickly.

EVERYTHING is ever-evolving. There is absolutely no such thing as an instantaneous perfect idea or success.

No creature is born in it's 'adult' form. We must bust unceremoniously out of our embryonic protection, depend on others for survival for a little while, figure out how to communicate, stay alive; we stumble and bumble our way through figuring out how to walk and hold things and eventually (sort of) find our place in the world - and with every passing moment we change, adapt and alter a little more.

Everything has to be trialled, tested, tweaked, iterated and improved as it is passes through the passage of time.

So PLEASE don't beat yourself up or hold your great self back from the world because you don't know what the view is like over the hill. That is like beating up a baby for not knowing what it wants to be when it's grown up. Harsh, but true.

Are you waiting for an epiphany, or some magical gift from the Universe to come and save you? If so, you will have a long and futile wait. I hate to tell you, but the epiphany isn't coming to change your life. No magical thought will mysteriously give you all the answers. That hope is worse than an illusion – it's a bold-faced lie!

Edison didn't just *invent* the light bulb.

Jobs didn't just *build* a MAC computer.

Every single great idea, every great business, every brilliant life is the result of years of vision, dedication, hard work, and progressive evolution. Your skills are a synthesis of all that you've done with your whole life.

Successful entrepreneurs don't get that way by just setting up a bank account, and BOOM! They are running a successful company. That does not happen.

If you intend to start creating courses or building an education-based business, you can't afford to sit there, waiting for 'your thing' to be revealed.

The perfect idea, the perfect situation, the perfect solution? They don't exist!

Do **something**. That is the ONLY way to find your 'thing'. Every great creation has a point of conception, and then it evolves.

'*Nothing*' cannot evolve; but '*something*', however tiny, most definitely can.

Do something – anything!

Only then will you have any experiences, feelings or data to base your next step from.

You need to take step 1 before you can collect the key that will open the door of step 2. You'll learn what works and what doesn't. From that first bold step, you'll gain new competencies and knowledge, enabling you to improve your plan – until you get it right!

Too many people are trying to bust open door 1000 with key 1. Don't put yourself under that kind of pressure.

Take a little tiny step with whatever you have right now, and what's required for step 2 will begin to present itself, when and only when you start taking some practical action.

This stage is about realising that's it's totally OK if you don't know where you're going yet, and that you don't actually need to in order to start. Starting is all you need to do, with whatever you have right now, whatever you know right now and whatever feels right right now.

We live in a world of CONSTANT change and if what we offer does not change with it, we'll be hanging out with with the *Fail-saurus-rex* pretty quickly.

Every GREAT creation has a point of conception, and then it evolves.

'*Nothing*' cannot evolve; but '*something*', however tiny, most definitely can.

CHAPTER 2

Overcome Self-Doubt and The Inner Imposter

When I decided that I wanted to break my training away from behind the safe and controlled walls of the corporate classroom in order to share it with the world, i knew that it would involve getting known out there in the big wide world.

Secretly, part of my ego was even a little tantalised by the idea of attaining a degree of industry 'fame'.

But, along with the tummy-tickling excitement and fantasies of myself signing my autograph on books for my adoring fans, I also felt a sense of blood-draining dread at the realisation that I didn't know everything about my topic. Poop. Double poop.

My fantasies of victoriously holding an award above my head in front of a cheering crowd for having educated millions of people, suddenly turned into a nightmare of publicly being asked questions that I didn't know the answers to; of being put on the spot in interviews about words i didn't understand, or theories I couldn't unpack, or industry news that I was not updated enough on to report my view on, or other experts who would spotlight my weaknesses to keep me down a peg.

The internal horror movies played out endlessly in my mind and convinced me that I just wasn't good enough yet. I had to be more of an 'actual expert' first. Right now I was nobody. Nobody knew who i was. I hadn't victoriously held any awards awards above my head barr the swimming badge i got when i was 10 and nobody between here and Pluto actually cared either.

But then I remembered that 19 year old girl (me) who started a business years ago because she loved something, because she was good at something and because people needed that something.

I remembered how it felt when a student had told me for the first time *'Sarah, you changed my life'*. I imagined being able to make that impact to millions of lives and my fire roared up, my stubbornness kicked in and the overwhelming sense of imposter syndrome was burned out enough to not hold me back. It never ever went away, but reminding myself of my strengths, my purpose and what I DID have to give, instead of all of the things that I didn't, was enough to power me on a little more each day.

4 years later, I held multiple awards above my head on stages in front of cheering crowds, i got sore wrists signing endless books to my supportive and loving followers, and as I write the words on this page I currently have a heart full of indescribable joy at having over 9,000 students in over 130 countries enrolled on my training - ALL because I kept ONE thing in mind: we ALL have something to give.

As well as the obvious, a key point here is that sitting around and 'waiting' until you are successful is the biggest oxymoron ever. You cannot get a success of any kind until you do SOMETHING. Doing nothing means you'll never be a success.

People don't just wake up one morning with awards, books and followers. You have to START somewhere - and precisely where you are right now IS the starting point. Just do what you can with what you have right now and don't stop until that part of the journey has given you some clues as to what's next.

Imposter syndrome kicks in when we spend more time focussing on the things we don't have instead of all of the things that we do. Here is a simple fact: it is IMPOSSIBLE to know EVERYTHING about a topic.

There is so much information, science, data, opinions, studies, theories, ideas, discussions and more out there that it is a factual impossibility to keep up with and retain all of that information in our human heads.

Secondly, it all changes so rapidly, that even if we could retain it all, we'd never be able to replace the old with the new 'as it happens' anyway. So, we really need to stop putting so much pressure on ourselves to think that we should be.

Knowing everything and worrying about what we don't know is not what's important when it comes to educating and leading in our industry. Sharing what we DO know is.

You have a wealth of valuable content and expertise to share - even if you don't know what it is yet

You do have a message. You do have a course inside of you. In fact, I'd go as far as saying that you probably have many courses inside of you.

Try not to allow that mojo-bashing thought creep in that 'you can't because you don't know it all'. People are not going to pay you for what you don't know. They are going to pay you for what you do know. Students are not going to enrol in your course called *'Stuff I Haven't Figured out Yet'*. They are going to enroll in the courses packed full of all of the knowledge you do have.

People are not going to praise you or give you awards for worrying about what you don't know, only for what you do.

So, what DO you know? Let's start with that....

You are brimming with expertise that others need

When our course creation mojo is taking a hit, we can all too easily convince ourselves that we don't have anything of value to give to others. We allow the media to consume us with the notion that we have to be someone famous, qualified or who has overcome some spectacular and newsworthy odds in order to consider ourselves as having anything worthy of listening to. But this of course is codswallop. EVERYONE has an abundance of valuable information packed into every cell of their body that has the power to change someone else's life, if only they would share it.

However old you are right now, THAT is how many years you have been training for your 'job' today. That is how much preparation and training life has given you to make you ready for the next part of your life.

You have learned SO many things. Skills, knowledge and life lessons are within you in abundance, that much is true.

You have learned things formally and informally, you have learned through work and through the highs and lows that life has presented to you. You have expertise that other people don't have yet. It could be cooking, communicating, a professional skill, an academic skill, a passionate hobby that you love encouraging others to try or a unique talent - all of which I can guarantee you that there are other people out there in the world that don't have those yet, and want to.

There are more than 7.2 billion people on earth, I'd put my last glass of my favourite wine down as a bet that at least a few of them would want to know what you know, and would want to do what you can do, no matter how small it may seem to you.

You may have been through experiences, good and bad, that have made you tougher, stronger, wiser, more cautious, more thorough, and more 'pro'. I bet that there are other people out there in the world who are at the beginning stages of a similar experience, or indeed in the midst of it and they are lost in the confusion with no idea what to do next, how to move on or how to break free. But you do.

You have the answer, or at least one of the answers. You have been there. You have been through a similar experience and if you really sat back and thought about it, you would be able to list a bunch of strategies that you didn't realise that you used and then share them with these people to help them get through that thing too.

Do not underestimate just how much you can help someone by just letting them know that they are not alone, that you have been there too, that you got through it, and that you would like to share the solutions and strategies that you used to move through that experience and get to where you are today.

You are so well equipped, you have so much on offer and there are so many people who need you to get over your fears, push away your imposter syndrome and step up with confidence in the power that you behold to make a difference to others with the gift of the learning that your life has provided for you.

> **ACTIVITY:**
> 1. What gift could you share?
> 2. What experiences have you overcome that you could help others get through (good and bad?)

List at least 50 skills, knowledge and expertise that you have that you could give other people even just one tip on

So ultimately, we must understand that imposter syndrome cannot be totally obliterated. In fact, now that I have got myself 'out there' and have put myself on that pedestal as an 'expert', I have to admit that the tendency for the self doubt to creep back in can actually increase. Its as if the devil on the proverbial shoulder now starts adding a whole other level of mojo-bashing whispers into our ears when we have 'made it'.

In the darkness of the night that little voice creeps in and says *'Hey Sarah, you know if they find you out NOW, after ALL of this, you are going to look even worse if you drop the ball?*

You know Sarah, NOW you actually have a reputation to lose, if they figure out that you are just an everyday girl hustling and grinding like everyone else is you're going to be busted, right?

What will they think Sarah, if now after calling yourself an expert, people see that there is stuff you don't know, because unlike before, now everyone is watching you?'

Its fascinating for me that no matter where we get to, or how high we go, we still have to find ways of dealing with the self doubts that come with putting ourselves out to the world from time to time.

And that's the point, this is an exercise not in getting rid of it, but learning how to push through it when it does pop up in our lives as an edupreneur.

CHAPTER 3

Overcoming Imposter Syndrome

You're about to press 'publish' on that online course, and all of a sudden you feel that surge of nausea creep up from the pit of your stomach and a little whisper starts telling you that maybe you should 'wait'. Maybe you should do some more research, or get more famous, or get a few more followers on your social media, or wait until you have an award or some other crazy thought that ultimately makes you stop.

The imposter syndrome.

The feeling of fraud.

We've all had a visit from her at some point. And this is because the very power of the authority pedestal makes those who have already placed themselves upon it, seem so great in their royal throne, that we immediately compare our knowledgeable crown jewels to theirs and think we can't compete unless we are wearing the very same ones.

Note that there are two key mojo-killers right here:

1. Comparing yourself to others
2. Assuming that someone else must put us in the 'expert' category in order to be worthy of having such a title

If we want to make ourselves seen as an expert, it starts with us calling ourselves one - not anyone else.

Many people cannot see a truth as evident, until it actually is. As in, until something IS a fact in their eyes, as evidenced by something that they can, hear and touch, then they find it very hard to see that it exists at all; so we have to SHOW them that we are an expert.

Gaining expert status requires YOU to give it to yourself, and YOU then have to go about proving that you are by acting as that expert.

You build your own throne, you don't get given it.

It never ceases to amaze me how many entrepreneurs I speak to who are dreaming of making a positive difference in the world, but never seem to get off of the starting line in making it happen.

When I ask them why they haven't done anything substantial to get their message out there yet, I very often get the same list of replies:

"Well, I still have a lot of research to do", *"There are so many people out there already doing it that I haven't quite come with anything special or different enough to stand out yet"*, or *"I need to wait until I'm seen as an expert before I go out there and start acting like one"*…

These are the exact same things I used to tell myself, and as a result, I wasted YEARS of helping others and living the life of my dreams.

You see, it's actually the most intelligent people that doubt themselves the most. For their intelligence, knowledge and insight has allowed them the wisdom that there is actually SO much more that they don't yet know. And so they focus on the limitations of their knowledge instead of their already existing abundance of it.

You are an expert.

So many highly experienced, talented, skilled and knowledgeable professionals and entrepreneurs never get themselves 'out there' or helping the world, because of the feeling of 'fraud' that they carry around with them. It's like the word 'expert' comes engraved onto a 20-tonne medallion that we have to carry around with us to 'prove' that it's true.

It scares people, and as a result, there are so many entrepreneurs out there who are not making enough money, working endlessly hard yet getting nowhere and have so much to give to their market but are getting drowned out by all the noise and overwhelm of competing with those they deem as 'better' than them.

But you don't need to compete. When you accept the fact that you ARE an expert, all you need to do is tell people what you know. Teach them how they can know it and do it too. That's it!

Here are 8 ways that you can start moving from a self-doubter, to an expert difference-maker:

1. Remember that you DO have a message. You already know SO much and this knowledge you have is invaluable to others; it has the power to transform lives, businesses and industries – as well as your own business and bottom line; if only you'd just unleash it!

2. Be aware that downloading your knowledge from your brain, and sharing it with others is THE highest converting method of building a strong and viable business. This is the true essence of 'edupreneurship'; educating, in a commercially profitable manner. It's business, where everyone's a winner.

3. Make the most of what you do have NOW – you can share what else you learn later on. Don't think you have to wait until you have the perfect recipe, or have attained ALL of the knowledge on planet earth in your topic. First of all, not only is that entirely impossible, but you couldn't share it all in one blog post, workshop or tutorial video anyway. Just go with what you've already got, as it's more than some people have.

4. Ask yourself whether you got to where you are in your life today, having not learnt ANYTHING? Of course you have. Start by listing 100 things that you think other people should know. Whatever comes to you head.

It could be something you discovered yourself in practice; something you read about or saw on TV; it could be something you heard someone else talk about – anything; personal and/or professional.

5. Break your knowledge down into micro topics and share it in multiple forms (blogs, videos, articles, audios, webinars etc) piece by piece. If you missed something out, or learn something new about that topic later, then do a new or updated post.

6. Know that you don't have to be a globally proclaimed celebrity authority expert in something to have value, information and worthiness to give, share and help others with. You simply have to share information about what you DO know how to do, to someone who doesn't yet know how to do that. It's a big world, so your chances of finding a few are pretty high.

7. Regularly remind yourself that you've learnt a lot in your life. Probably most through your mishaps and the times things have gone wrong. There are a ton of people out there that are yet to make those mistakes, or trip on those mishaps and are yet to learn the things you have learned, whether you learned them formally or through experience. You are doing a selfish disservice to those people if you don't share your lessons with others.

8. Attain a sense of responsibility that it's your job and your purpose in the world, to help people that don't know it yet to know it; and to help them

use that knowledge to make their lives and their businesses better.

Be the edupreneur – make positive change – profitably!

Educating and informing others in your industry topic automatically positions you as the good guy, the helper, the GURU in what you do.

Disseminating helpful information makes people love you, like you, want more from you, become grateful to you – AND want to pay you for more.

Everyone has a message. Everyone has some kind of expertise within them.

We all have a degree of knowledge and skills that can be shared to make us the authority in our field; to make a lot more money and to make a big impact on our markets.

All we have to do is see our own expertise as a valuable and saleable resource that is needed by others. Goodbye imposter mojo-killer.

Share Your Own Way

Being an expert isn't about memorising the way other people do things, or what it says in a guide book elsewhere. It's more about having your own viewpoint, your own methodology and your own unique approach to a common problem.

Remembering this is a great way to beat the internal feeling of fraud. If you have achieved success in something, you have survived through a certain kind of experience or pulled through a particular situation, you can teach HOW you personally overcame that situation or got the results that you got.

Using the phrase *'this is what worked for me when i did XYZ and got ABC result'* shows that you have evidence of success and have the strategies to share with others so that they can attempt to implement and replicate your outcomes too.

This takes you away from now comparing yourself to others and instead making yourself unique, different and exclusively expert in your own methodology. Nobody can say you are wrong, incorrect or insufficient in your explanation, because you are basing your training on what YOU did, how YOU see it and what YOU have used yourself to get YOUR unique results.

As a real example, I am no 'expert' in book publishing in the sense that that it is not my qualified profession, but at the time of writing this I have successfully self-published 3 books and got all of them to number one spots on Amazon internationally. A lot of people began asking me how i did it, and so I created an online course called '*Sarah's Amazon Best-Seller Success Strategies*' and opened my welcome video with the lines '*I'm not claiming to be an expert in publishing, but in this course I will simply share with you precisely what steps I took to write, publish and get my books to number one so that you can copy them*'.

That way I immediately removed any concern of backlash from the publishing industry or worry about whether anyone would criticise me as a 'non-publishing expert', because it was simply a course on '*how I do it*'.

> You BUILD your own throne, you don't get given it.

It's actually the *most intelligent* people that doubt themselves the most. For their intelligence, knowledge and insight has allowed them the wisdom that there is actually SO much more that they don't yet know. And so they focus on the limitations of their knowledge instead of their already existing abundance of it.

Everyone has a message. Everyone has some kind of expertise within them.

We all have a degree of KNOWLEDGE and SKILLS that can be shared to make us the authority in our field; to make a lot more *money* and to make a *big impact* on our markets.

All we have to do is see our OWN EXPERTISE as a valuable and saleable resource that is needed by others.

Being an expert isn't about memorising the way other people do things, or what it says in a guide book elsewhere. It's more about having your OWN viewpoint, your OWN methodology and your OWN unique approach to a common problem.

CHAPTER 4

Healthy Fear,
Or
Out of Alignment?

There is a difference between being afraid and being totally out of alignment.

Putting yourself out to the world, especially if this is your first time, is scary- and i'd even go as far as saying that if you don't have the teeniest, tiniest bit of apprehension then maybe you don't care enough. Fear is healthy. Fear makes you check and double check that you are delivering to the best of your abilities. Fear makes us stop for a moment and check that we are delivering something we are truly proud of.

However, if we are feeling dread, agonising despair, if we are feeling like the whole process is a painful drag and something we simply don't enjoy or have any excitement for whatsoever, then it's likely we are going down the wrong path entirely and perhaps should reconsider where the source of our self-doubt is coming from.

Find and address the source of your fears and ask yourself 'do they actually have anything to do with course creation, or are they about something else?'

CHAPTER 5

What To Do If The Worst Happens

Sometimes - just sometimes, our biggest fears, the things we are most afraid of can actually happen.

For me, the single best way of overcoming this feeling of 'being rubbish and not good enough' is to over-deliver, over-help and be the kindest, most useful person anyone has ever come across. And honestly, i immediately feel better about everything from my skills and knowledge to my entire existence.

When I feel down about my abilities, I go out of my way to FIND people that i can help. I look for questions that I can answer in Facebook groups, I scroll through forums and seek questions being asked specifically on things I know how to do.

There is no greater affirmation of your innate abilities than showing yourself that you have a tonne of answers to questions other people are asking, and for them to thank you for the information and enlightenment.

In fact, it is my moments of complete self-doubt that have actually caused the greatest shifts in my success.

In early 2016 I gave birth to my long awaited baby daughter, Chloe. As much as my husband and I had been trying to bring her into the world for 3 years and i longed for her with every ounce of my being, I was still terrified about how I was going to cope with upholding my professional castle, whilst adjusting to my new role of 'mummy', especially since we had no family whatsoever on the same side of planet earth as us.

I was on edge, my self-efficacy was crumbling and i was very very afraid.

There has never been a time in my life where i felt more like 'I cant do this'. And then, the absolute worst happened. Just as I was holding my newborn baby in my arms, my company got its first ever unhappy customer in over a decade. To add an extra layer of horrifying terror to the already soul-crushing situation, said unhappy customer immediately went on an almighty and entirely overactive public tirade about the ugly powerpoint presentation she had received (it was pretty ugly).

In business we all have to deal with the crazy customers, but to have your first one in a decade at the same time as already dealing with self-doubt AND having your hands spectacularly tied by a bundle of love at 3am on a Saturday night when you literally cannot do anything to resolve the situation, can really push a girl over the edge! This situation literally threw me into the hormone fuelled grasp of severe anxiety as I read her hate mail and public abuse (even after I had given her a full refund!).

Afterall, i had told the world i was an expert. I had categorised myself as the best in the business. I had positioned myself, my company and my team as spectacular. I had built a following of wonderful supporters who believed me as I had believed myself from a decade of successful results. For anyone who's course creation and edupreneurial mojo is feeling a little distant, this experience was for me the equivalent of it combusting into a cataclysmic scatter bomb and taking my soul into hell with it's own remains. Dramatic?

Yes. True? Most certainly.

But here's where it gets interesting and why I can now look back at this situation and wish that I could thank this customer for what has turned into one of the biggest turning points to the rise of my most recent success. After overcoming my initial reaction to run, hide and give up, I took stock of the facts.

If you ever find yourself in a similar situation, reflect on the following:

1. Remember why you started
2. Remember what you love
3. Remember all of the people over the years that you have helped
4. Remember that you DO know a metric tonne of stuff that is super helpful to others
5. Remember that you can make a positive difference to more people
6. Remember that you are a good person

I went through these reflections myself and came to one conclusion:

All I have to do is keep proving it.

To keep proving it, all I have to do is serve, give and help.

Nobody hates a helpful giver.

I was so worried that this person's comments to others would damage my name and my work (yes I gave ONE person this much power in a time that I was weak), that I decided the only way I could recover was to show the entire world to just how wrong this customer was.

I imagined her saying to someone *'That Sarah is rubbish'*, and then imagined that the people she was saying it to simply looking at her like she was bonkers whilst presenting to her a million ways that i had helped them and helped others.

Achieving this meant more than telling people that my company and i were great at what we did. It meant more than fighting her tirade. It actually meant forgetting her altogether and going full-throttle into my *'do what i came onto earth to accomplish'* mission.

She thought that discrediting someone was to say unjustified mean things about them. All I had to do to counter her unjustified opinion was to make it just that - by PROVING through the act of undeniable, factual, quantifiable evidence that I was none of the things I was imagining that she might have been saying about me in the big easily influenced world.

I tapped into my inner knowledge vault. I shared and shared and shared. I helped and helped and helped. I went out of my way to serve others. I created streams of blog posts, articles, videos, courses, spoke at events for free, gave my knowledge and advice freely and made an absolute point of being the leading edupreneur that I'd promised myself, my team and my industry that I was.

I have to admit, that all of this initially derived from a

place of survival. From a starting point of fear - but the real 'happy ending' and immense learning outcome from this story was about to present itself….

Suddenly, the messages of gratitude began flooding in. My inbox became inundated with with people saying how much my content had been helping them. My course sales went up dramatically, my following increased by more than 3,000% in just a couple of months, we couldn't keep up with the enquiries and business and I had to hire 5 new people as well as turn business away. My notifications of people tagging me in Facebook groups as 'the guru' in my field were out of control, i was being approached by podcasters and conference organisers to speak for their audiences and before i knew it, the place i thought i'd lost really was gone - now i was a heap of levels higher than before the entire debacle even started.

The power of giving had just shown itself to me in ways I could never have expected.

I was forced into an internal sense of urgency to SHOW the world what i had, what i could do, who i was and what i cared about and i did it without reservation.

The results of giving my knowledge away and showing people that i could help them not only made the whole thing fizzle out and improve my business; but believe it or not also made the woman in question get back in touch a few months later and apologise profusely for her 'unprofessional reaction' and actually say the words *'because it's evident from everything you've been doing just how much you care about your customers and how good you are at what you do, I'm sorry'*. As I responded with genuine gratitude to this customer, I suddenly realised that having a delicate mojo was actually the very essence of my strength.

And do you know what, it's yours too.

I always believed in 'giving is getting', and have always been a 'speculate to accumulate' kind of entrepreneur. But this experience showed me unequivocally, that the more you give, the more *everyone* gets.

ACTIVITY:

1. What do you care about?
2. What are you worried about?
3. Are you delivering as much help as you could be?
4. How can you level up how much help you give to the world?

There is no greater affirmation of your innate abilities than SHOWING YOURSELF that you have a tonne of answers to questions other people are asking, and for them to thank you for the information and enlightenment.

CHAPTER 6

But My Family, Friends & Dog Say I shouldn't Do It

For many people, what other people think about them is really important - especially those that they love. Getting support and approval from the people we care about the most can be hugely important and for many people, the ultimate deciding factor about whether they go ahead with what they were thinking about doing or not. It's totally normal.

I often tell the story of how I first started out in business. Brimming with fresh excitement and an untainted ego, I couldn't wait to tell my partner at the time, and my mum what i had planned for the world.

It was a freezing winter's day in the UK. The kind with sideways rain and pitch blackness by 3pm. But this was a day I didn't notice the misery. I excitedly ran home to tell my partner at the time 'I'm going to be an entrepreneur!!'

He paused his TV show, smiled at me, and said *"Don't come crying to me when it all goes wrong!"*.

Ouch.

Annoyed but not deterred I drove to my mums house as fast as I could and excitedly told her *'mum mum mum, I'm going to be an entrepreneur!!'* She took a long puff on her cigarette and squawked *"What the bloody hell is wrong with you Sarah? Get your head out of the clouds and get a real job! And don't come crying to me when it all goes wrong!"*

I was hurt. I cared deeply about having the support of those closest to me. I momentarily considered backing out. Maybe they were right? Was I being stupid?

I was about to embark on an alien journey, and I knew I was going to have to face it not only without the help and support of those around me, but with their active disapproval dragging me backwards too.

As much as the mountain felt insurmountable, a fire burned inside of me so defiantly, that even the icey downpour from my family couldn't put it out. I forged ahead and started climbing it alone regardless.

Over a decade on from that day, I had gone on to run my education business in 3 different countries, had employed over 50 full time staff, hundreds of contractors, been the catalyst of the education of thousands of people globally and had built an asset worth millions of dollars.

Needless to say, my mum is now my BIGGEST fan - and my ex is totally kicking himself!

The point is, that not everybody is like us edupreneurs. Not everyone has the ability to see beyond the tangible into what could be possible, and therefore they assume that anything not physically measurable simply does not, or cannot exist.

The Three Stages of Recognising 'Truth'

Arthur Schopenhauer tells us that all truths pass through 3 stages before being accepted.

Stage 1

First, the new idea is ridiculed. People who cannot believe that something is possible will immediately react by laughing and poking fun at it. It seems so impossible to them that it seems 'silly' to them, quite literally in the sense of being absurd. This doesn't mean it actually is absurd however, it just means that their literal mindset cannot fathom the materialisation of something they do not understand.

Stage 2

The second stage a truth will pass through is 'opposition'.

Often the idea is violently opposed. They'll say, *'That can't be done.'* or *'Why fix something that isn't broken?'* This is because when people cannot fathom a concept, to protect themselves from looking short sighted, they will defend their viewpoint by trying to assert to you how they think your idea won't and cannot work. By coming up with reasons why you could fail, they are internally justifying their own inability to conceptualise your vision; not necessarily passing judgement on your capability to actualise it.

But for those like the 19 year old me, who don't give up in the face of ridicule and violent opposition, a third phase will be experienced.

Stage 3

In the third stage, the new 'truth' (your idea) is accepted as self-evident.

For example, if the dream was to train to run a marathon, at first your loved ones might ridicule and oppose your dream:

'You can't run a marathon, You're fat!' 'You couldn't even run a bath!'.

But you trained anyway. You put all of your effort in, you worked hard and eventually, you ran that marathon!

Whether your loved ones were standing at the finish line or not, it would now a be an evident fact that you 'run marathons' and they would accept that fact, whether they support it or not.

My mother is now my biggest fan; she proudly announces to anyone who will listen that her daughter is a successful entrepreneur. She can't even remember those times when she doubted me. My success is just accepted as evident now.

As much as the mountain felt insurmountable, a fire burned inside of me so defiantly, that even the icey downpour from my family couldn't put it out. I forged ahead and STARTED CLIMBING it alone regardless.

CHAPTER 7

Dealing With Your 'Non-Supporters'

Non-Supporter Type 1

When we find ourselves faced with loved ones, friends and even entire communities who doubt us, ridicule us or just simply don't seem as supportive as we'd like them to be about our edupreneurial ideas, just remember that leaders, innovators, and entrepreneurs see the world differently to that way that the rest of the population do.

We are visionary and futuristic in our very nature. We see things that don't yet exist. This frustrates our friends, neighbours, and even our colleagues.

Most have no intention of being unsupportive, but the way they are genetically wired quite literally makes it impossible for them to visualise or conceptualise something that doesn't yet exist. It's not their fault and you can't 'train it into them'. Many simply don't have that futuristic characteristic within them and never will.

So although it hurts when those around you are unsupportive, try not to get angry at them, as it's less about their belief in you and simply a lack of the futuristic characteristic that you are so lucky to have.

Non-Supporter Type 2

The second kind of 'non-supporter' is the one who really really loves you and wants to protect you from failure because seeing you hurt or upset would be devastating for them. These people also lack the futuristic characteristic, and because they cannot see how such a dream could be accomplished, they assume failure is inevitable.

Because they care about you so much, they will try to talk you 'out of it' or dampen your idea in whichever ways they can.

As much as this can be infuriating and heart breaking, when faced with this kind of treatment we need to remember that these people are coming from a place of love.

Recognise it, thank them for caring about you and do it anyway.

Non-Supporter Type 3

Some people are unsupportive because they don't share our vision or they disagree with our beliefs.

Your job as an edupreneur is to share with the world what you believe in. To build a tribe of people that you can serve who are on the same mission and pathway as you.

With this in mind, don't worry about the people who disagree with you - you are not here to please them. You only need to focus on the people who *do* like and agree with you and have similar beliefs.

It's not your job to convert non-believers. It's your job to serve those who already are.

Non-Supporter Type 4

Then there are people who are not so much concerned about the activity you plan to get stuck into, but are terrified that THEIR world will change if you succeed. Many people, particularly the non-entrepreneurial type, are very resistant to change, and they are even more resistant to step into the unknown.

What if you succeed and it changes their world?

What if you behave differently, get new friends, have a new routine?

These people will doubt you, oppose you and give you every reason why your idea is 'stupid' and a waste of time - anything to try to keep their world 'safe' and predictable.

Reassure them that you will still be there and care for them.

Tell them not to worry and that everything will be ok because you have them beside you; and then go on and do it.

Non-Supporter Type 5

Some people are unsupportive because they are envious.

Many people cannot see that a self-directed life of freedom is possible for them and their jealousy gets the better of them, spilling onto you as hatred or aggression.

There isn't much that you can do about the way others feel about their own lives. You certainly should not allow someone else's reflection to fog up yours.

You could share your journey with them and show them that they can have it too; but you'd possibly be wasting your time, as deeply jealous people would even see your offer of help as an insulting attempt to 'rub salt into their wounds'.

Send them a wish of hope and luck and carry on with your mission.

Non-Supporter Type 6

Finally, some people are unsupportive quite simply because they are butt-holes. In the same way that you 'cannot polish a turd', don't try to win over the butt-hole that it came out of either. Step away from the toilet, take whatever poop they have thrown at you and use it to nourish and fertilise your own beautiful meadows. You've got a world to change after all.

If you are determined to succeed, be ready for these oppositional mindsets. You can't let it offend you. You see the world differently. You have a calling that they don't have, and a fire in your belly that will take you places they don't even dream of!

CHAPTER 8

I've Got More Planning & Research To Do First

Yes. Great courses have been well researched and are brimming with useful, implementable and factually correct information. So of course a bit of research is going to be on the cards for all of us edupreneurs.

However, way too many edupreneurs use this stage as the perfect procrastination station.

They get off of the course creation train here and they stop for a lifetime using the '*i need to do more research first*' excuse until the next century.

9 times out of 10, anyone using these words is simply procrastinating (sorry).

One of my clients and now friends, Gail, came to my home in Western Australia in early 2017 for a one on one school set up and course filming day with me.

The night before our session, she rang me and said, '*Sarah I am going to have to reschedule our session tomorrow, as I am not ready and still have a huge amount of research to do first*'. I let her finish and quite simply replied with '*No. See you tomorrow*'.

You see, I knew from one quick skype call that Gail knew her topic inside out. She told me she'd been 'doing it for years' and that she never stops giving people advice on her topic - which is exactly why she wanted to turn it into an online course.

She was tired of 'going for coffee' so that people could 'pick her brains' for free.

She was tired of so many people saying they wanted to come to her workshops but not being able to charge enough to cover the costs of the physical training venue; she was tired of everyone saying they wanted to attend her workshops but never being able to find a day when everyone could attend them around their own life commitments.

She clearly had a skill that people wanted and she clearly had a lot of experience sharing it. She needed to get these online - but as soon as the reality of this new journey presented itself, a little bit of overwhelm, a bit of procrastination, and perhaps a little bit of fear all crept in and told her *'you don't know enough, wait, stay back, don't move'*.

But for Gail, there was no 'get out of jail free card', because she had hired me to make her online course come to life, and that was precisely what she was going to get. '*No*' I said unquestionably back down the phone.

Gail paused for a moment and I heard her heart beating through the receiver. *'You see Gail'* I told her. *'You already know everything that you know'*. *'Yea but'*, she jumped in with a panicky tone. *'Yea but nothing Gail. You are not coming to my house tomorrow to teach a course on stuff you don't know, are you?' 'Well no'*, she said, now sounding a little more certain. *'So why do you need to do more research?'* I asked. She fell silent for a moment so I continued. *'You are coming to my house tomorrow to teach what you DO already know Gail. You are NOT coming here to teach what you don't know. Who comes to you and asks you to go for coffee to pick your brain about things you don't know? Who wants to come on your workshop called 'The Workshop About Everything Gail Doesn't Know'? Nobody right? You are going to be teaching what you know, and that's it. If you don't know it yet, then you shouldn't be teaching it. Save it for when you do know it, and then guess what? You can add it to your course later and give your students the benefit of 'lifetime upgrades' in doing so'*.

I felt Gail's whole body relax in the breath she let out at that moment. *'The only thing you need to do tonight Gail, is have a nice hot bath, get a good night's sleep and get ready for me to pull everything that you already know out of your head into your course plan for you tomorrow. I'll see you at 9am'.*

The next day Gail absolutely smashed her online course. She stopped thinking about all of the things she didn't know, and only focussed on what she did.

We produced her course plan in 3 hours and she then filmed her entire online course in the afternoon. She has since come back and coached other clients of mine experiencing the same panic that she initially did on their filming days. Magic.

When you are in this space, remember that perfectionism will kill you. You do not need an academic journal and university funded research team behind you to make a great online course. You only need to remember that the audience you are targeting are the ones that *don't* know your stuff yet. That the entire reason they are taking your course.

If you are creating a course on healthy eating, don't write it for the PHD Nutritionist with 50 years experience. Write it for the person that is most like you were when you needed the advice that you're about to share.

Don't make yourself feel overwhelmed worrying about every single piece of knowledge that exists in the world of nutrition! It would be an actual impossibility to know everything in your industry. Only worry about what you do know right now and share that.

It's Never Final

The best thing about online learning is that you can change, add and adapt any of your content as many times as you like, at any time really easily.

My own online courses are never ever finished. I forver add to them.

Everytime i read a book or an article and come across a new tip that will fit into a course, I film a new video or write up a text lecture and add it in.

If someone asks a great question in the course, I'll film a new video with the answer and add it in as a new lecture. It's not only a great way to overcome the overwhelm, but also makes a great excuse to keep adding value to your students journey and your programs. After a while I increase the price of my courses because I've added so much new content to it since its original publish date.

Also remember that procrastinating, researching and planning does not help ANYONE, it doesn't help you either. The only thing that can help people is getting your content to them. So get it to them. You can update it later if you come across that 'oh so desired' piece of research that you seek. Keep in mind that the number one thing that people want is the *how-to tip*, the strategy, the 'what do i need to do' answer they are looking for. Although highly valuable and important (especially to the left brain learner) the case studies and statistics and so on ultimately come second. Remember that the crux of your program is about helping your learner to get the results that they need, and I'm not sure if a well researched statistic has ever been behind any of my greatest successes if I'm honest.

Finally, always do your research AFTER you have your draft course plan together (yes DRAFT - nothing is ever final).

A course evolves as it's being built, even if you do start with having super clear outcomes.

If you start researching as you are designing your course plan, you could risk researching information that is totally irrelevant or waste time gathering information that may not even be included in your final version of your course.

I go into much more detail of the course creation process in my book '*Entrepreneur to Edupreneur*', but the best way to begin your course creation in terms of when to do your research is as follows:

1. Compile your overall aims, objectives and outcomes

2. Write down everything that you already know that relates to the outcomes in 'short tip form'

3. Put your tips in a progressive order of modules and lectures

4. Remove any irrelevant tips and information and add it to the 'save for another course' pile

5. Compose the content that you already know

6. THEN do any research to see what else you can find that you already know, that will contribute to what you already have.

Have your objectives and learning outcomes clearly placed in front of you when you start you research phase and make sure that you are searching for something specific to illustrate, back-up or ensure the delivery of that outcome. Random browsing is bad for course creation mojos.

Make sure that your research is even required in the first place. Too many edupreneurs research for the sake of 'seeing if they can find 'stuff'' and just start collecting random piles of information that lead them off into a bottomless maze of wormholes. The information must directly support the tip being given or the outcome being sought; or it's just fluff.

For each tip, piece of information and content that you are giving, ask yourself *'does this really need anything else added to it, or am I going over and beyond what's required by adding anything further to this?'*.

Online courses are not about showing how much you know, trying to look smart or playing in some silent competition to 'have the most content'. They are about delivering the outcome to the learner as thoroughly and valuably as possible in the most straightforward yet engaging route there is.

If what you are researching directly contributes to achieving a learning outcome for the learner, then most certainly include it. If it contributes to the learning process by opening up that content to different learning preferences or information processing styles, then include it.

If it's simply taking up space, either leave it out altogether or create a 'Bonus' section of additional reading in a bonus module so that's it's clear that it's not a required part of the course, but is available for those who like to have more research information and further reading at their fingertips should they wish to consume the 'over and above' information.

If you find yourself at this procrastination station, remember that you truly could be researching for your entire life. Just get what you do know out there right away, and add new research as you do it later.

The time is now, people need you and what you already have right now. That's all you need to share.

Perfectionism will kill you. You do not need an academic journal and university funded research team behind you to make a great online course. You ONLY NEED to remember that the audience you are targeting are the ones that don't know your stuff yet. That the entire reason they are taking your course.

The best thing about online learning is that you CAN CHANGE, add and adapt any of your content as many times as you like, at any time really easily.

Remember that the crux of your program is about helping your learner to get the results that they need, and I'm not sure if a well researched statistic has ever been behind any of my greatest successes if I'm honest.

- Compile your overall aims, objectives and outcomes
- Write down everything that you already know that relates to the outcomes in 'short tip form'
- Put your tips in a progressive order of modules and lectures
- Remove any irrelevant tips and information and add it to the 'save for another course' pile
- Compose the content that you already know
- THEN do any research to see what else you can find that you already know, that will contribute to what you already have.

Have your objectives and learning outcomes clearly placed in front of you when you start you research phase and make sure that you are searching for something specific to illustrate, back-up or ensure the delivery of that outcome. Random browsing is bad for course creation mojos.

If what you are researching directly contributes to achieving a learning outcome for the learner, then most certainly include it. If it contributes to the learning process by opening up that content to different learning preferences or information processing styles, then include it.

CHAPTER 9

I'm Not Clear On Why I'm Doing This

I once got thrown out of a history class for asking my teacher 'what the point was' of his lesson. If as adults, we cannot clearly see the purpose, relevance or meaning behind something we are doing, then our motivation will be extremely short lived and completion of the task in question will be unlikely.

Not only will our students be asking you what the point is in taking your course - but YOU need to begin the entire process by asking yourself the same question.

What's the point of creating your course?

If you are *only* in this for the money, you should probably pack up your tool box now and find something else to do - this industry requires a whole lot of love if you want to survive, let alone be successful.

You need to uncover what's beneath that need for cash and then decide if this is the best path to obtain that for you.

Creating and selling online courses isn't all 'lights, camera, action' and laptops on beaches. In fact, it's hard work and sometimes very challenging. Even if your courses do start earning you the big bucks, I can categorically assure you that it's not the money that'll keep you getting up in the mornings when you're pushing through one of the harder times in edupreneur life.

The key to success as an edupreneur is being absolutely passionate about what you do and having a driving sense of purpose behind you. It's about knowing your 'edupreneurial why'.

Now this doesn't necessarily need to mean, knowing the purpose of your life, or your career direction or having a clear idea of even what your real 'thing' is as such.

I truly believe that you can still be really successful whilst still trying to find that out.

However, when it comes to course creation, you do need to know why you are creating that course.

- Why teaching it is important to you.
- Why you want to invest your time and effort into producing it, marketing it, building a platform for it and giving your heart to your students.
- May be you are doing this to simply give back to world, to make a difference in some way to your industry, to be the person you wish you'd had when you started out.

Why do you want to create your course?

If you are doing this to earn money, or become famous in your industry, or because it's a great lead into another primary product or service you have, that's all great too - but make sure you delve down deeper into the 'why' you want the fame or the money in the first place.

- What emotion are you seeking from that fame or money?
- What change are you seeking in your own life or others lives from that fame or money?

Everything has a deeper reason, and you need to know

what these deeper reasons are for you if you are going to cut it and survive in this industry - coins in the pocket alone are not enough. Ask yourself why you want those coins and you'll begin to uncover that real 'why'. Your why is what will get you through. Quite simply, if your 'why' is big enough, then your TRY can be big enough.

The important thing is to get explicitly clear on that 'why', that reason, that purpose, so that you can design your course in a way that will be certain to achieve that (yes, course creation is as much about serving you as it is your students); and also to be sure that you have a powerful list of motivators to come back to if things get tough in the process.

Our 'why' needs to be much deeper than vague statements like *'to make the world a better place'*

Instead we must ask ourselves, WHY do we want to make the world a better place?

And then keep going until we get to the CORE of why doing that is important to us.

Vicktor Frankyl tells us that if man has meaning, he is able to push through any experience, any trauma and do so without faltering from his mission - if you know what your ultimate mission and vision is (even if only for this course) this will alone add endless fuel to your mojo. Nobody and nothing can take away your drive and motivation when you have a mission and vision that is much bigger than you.

ACTIVITY: Finding Your Course Creation 'Why'

Here are some questions to ask yourself to get clear on your 'why' for your online course:

1. The first method is to ask yourself 'why' 5 times, or until you get to an 'emotion' answer.

    The 5 whys method was originally stemmed from engineers in the Ford factories who wanted to find the root cause of defects and problems in the production process.

    We can replicate this method to find the 'root cause' of our our course.

    Why do you want to create this course? Write down your answer.

2. Then ask yourself 'why you want that?'
3. Then ask for a third time, 'why do you want that?' And so on, until you get to a really deep emotional answer. Get really specific. 'Feel happy' isn't enough. Why do you want to feel happy? Get a friend to challenge you and push you to go further. It may feel a little repetitive as you go around and explore, but every answer you give is really important in pulling out those drivers, motivators and reasons behind your course.

    What emotions and 'whys' did you ultimately end up at?

4. What is the bigger picture for you?
5. How will building this course help others?
6. How will building this course help your industry?
7. How will creating it help you financially?
8. How will it help you emotionally?
9. How will it contribute to the greater good?
10. What other motivating reasons can you list for creating your course?

CHAPTER 10

I Can't Afford To Do It

I work with many aspiring edupreneurs every week. All of them have great ideas and an abundance of talent that they could serve with and profit from.

When I ask them why they haven't started yet, a common response is 'I can't afford to'. It never fails to astound me that so many people think that they need to have to have an investor, or access to life savings to start a business. That's absolute, complete and utter baloney.

Of course it *helps* to have money, I'm not denying that it definitely makes the process easier, but I can categorically assure you that you don't NEED it to get started. This is yet another procrastination or fear-based tactic that your body is using to hold you back from your greatness.

The first reaction I get from many at this stage is '*yes but Sarah, it's alright for you to say that, you've got money*'. True. But i didn't start out with any.

In early March 2012, I landed in Western Australia with a 25 kg suitcase, a belly full of fear and excitement, and absolutely nothing else. Originally from the UK, and not knowing at that stage that you could sell a business, I'd quite literally shut down shop, packed up my stuff and got on a plane leaving everything I'd built behind me. (Yes it still hurts knowing that I could have sold it for quite a lot of money!). I stood outside the arrivals doors with my suitcase at Perth international airport, with the hot late summer air blowing through my hair, succumbing to the sudden realisation that I was quite literally broke, alone and homeless.

I knew absolutely nobody. I didn't know how business in

Australia went, and I definitely didn't have any cash behind me. I had no phone, no laptop, no job, nowhere to live, and no idea what the hell I was going to do. I didn't have a bed to sleep on, let alone any money in my pocket to buy one.

Yet after just 18 months of rocking up frightened and penniless, I had a business valued at millions of dollars.

Three years earlier, I had been in precisely the same position in Malta. On a whim, I had randomly packed up my life in the UK after a breakup. When I arrived in Malta, I was still extremely inexperienced in the world of business (especially in a foreign country that spoke a different language). And yet within two months I had a contract with the European Government, a national bank, an international top-end hotel chain and several national retail outlets. My starting budget? Nothing.

I don't have any magic trick to pull out of my hat for you. No secret formula, no super-powers of any kind. I'm an everyday person with a hole in my butt just like you.

The difference between me and those who don't ever get started, let alone succeed, is that I know that if I want to have something, then I must go and get it for myself, not wait around for someone to give it to me. I know that building a business with no money, contacts or internet connection is tough, but I also know that using that as an excuse to never realise my dreams will ultimately be tougher.

Everything I have today in my profession and in business came from mastering how to create something from nothing - and deliberately taking strategic action every day to go and get it.

If you have a bed, an internet connection and a mobile phone, you are already a million miles ahead of where i was when I started in Australia, and you've got everything you need.

In order to earn money, you need customers.

To get customers, they have to know that you exist.

The ONLY thing you need to show someone that you exist, is yourself. Your body, your voice and your smile. That's free.

Go to the local library - the internet, books, computers and often the odd page of printing is free.

Go to your local Chamber of Commerce and Industry, they often have free business training, consulting, legal and advisory services.

Search online for events, conferences, network meetings, seminars, workshops and expos in your subject niche and attend all of them that are free - the majority of them are. This is the best opportunity to grow your network.

You don't need fancy business cards with professionally designed logos on them. You just need yourself. People don't buy services based on a business card, they buy them based on the person who is selling the service.

In the first week of arriving in Australia, I knew that if I didn't get a client ASAP, i was going to very rapidly starve to death. And no, i'm not being dramatic, i was homeless and I had nothing to eat. I knew that it was critical to my survival to start letting people know that I exist, to start sharing with them how I can help them and what i can do for them to help them reach their goals and objectives. I walked around every free event i could get myself to. I 'acquired' a push bike (ok, I stole it from a verge collection) and i pushed my little legs along the freeway in the searing Australian heat to get myself to events that I knew were going to be packed with my target audience. Nothing was going to stop me getting a meal that week.

I didn't have business cards, I didn't have a logo, I didn't have a website, I hadn't even registered my business yet. But i had everything I needed. Myself, my voice and my passion for what I did.

I collected business cards, i went back to the library the next day, i sent out emails thanking people for their lovely conversations and i offered them my services. After 2 weeks, I had met and collected the cards of over 300 people. Within 3 months I had a 6 figure contract and had to hire 9 people to see it through.

I wrote to the conference organisers and offered to speak for free. Within a couple of months I was speaking on major stages to hundreds of people at a time, many of whom queued up afterwards to speak with me and invite me to consult their organisation - being on a stage gives you instant cred - and customers.

Soon enough I was getting referrals left, right and centre, I didn't even need to look for business anymore.

As soon as i got my first client, I used the income to pay for a website; my second contract bought my business cards, my third bought my laptop; and so it continued, until i was firmly established and operating like any other business does with 23 staff.

Even to this day, i find that the 'free' lead generation activities are my most profitable. I have spent only pennies on paid advertising. ALL of my traffic and work comes from doing things that anyone and everyone can do right now with an internet connection, determination and a belly full of guts.

ANYONE who tells me that they can't get started because of money is making excuses, it's that simple.

If you need to film videos but don't have filming gear, see if another course creator lives close to you and might lend you theirs. If not, do your filming from your mobile phone. Done is better than not done, even if it's not 'perfect'.

If you don't have a phone, ask a friend if you can borrow theirs to record your videos. If you don't have any friends, ask a stranger. You'll be amazed at what people will help you out with. When I finally got myself somewhere to live in Australia, my next door neighbours let me go into their house every single day to use their computer and do my washing. They even let me borrow cutlery and a kettle from their camper van until I could afford to get myself together. Ask for help, put a call out on Facebook, hustle, innovate, get creative, look for free services in your local area and offer to swap your services or plain elbow grease in return for a service you need. I still to this day swap services for services with people.

The old adage 'where there is a will, there is a way' couldn't be more true in my mind.

There are endless free tools, apps and platforms out there that can help you build your business without the need to spend a single cent.

Go to Udemy.com and find free courses and use YouTube to learn new skills so that you can do tasks yourself instead of paying someone else to do it.

You can build a website in 2 hours for free these days.

You can design your own logos and business cards for free.

You can host your online courses on marketplaces and LMSs for free, you can share your content in every single imaginable way for free.

You can build an audience for free, you can get published in books, blogs and magazines for free, you can appear in podcasts for free.

The list goes on and on.

In today's world of resources, you have absolutely no excuse for not getting your edupreneurial business off of the ground.

You already have ALL of the resources that you need to do what you want to do and get your message out to the world. No money? No problem. You don't need any.

I know that BUILDING A BUSINESS with no money, contacts or internet connection is tough, but I also know that using that as an excuse to never realise my dreams will ultimately be tougher.

In order to earn money, you need customers.

To get customers, they have to know that you exist.

The ONLY thing you need to show someone that you exist, is yourself.

Your body, your voice and your smile.

THAT'S FREE.

CHAPTER 11

I Don't Have Enough Time

Most business owners, entrepreneurs, in fact , anyone i meet want two things: more money and more time freedom.

Online courses, when done correctly and in conjunction with a proper entrepreneurial business plan can give you both more time and more money - let alone all of the other benefits of impacting more people, contributing to an industry, an economy and a movement that advances humanity in some way.

Yet bizarrely i find time and time again that the very thing that can help people get them exactly what they want, is the thing that they put to the bottom of their priority list over and over again - creating their online courses!

The irony of this is that anyone saying that they don't have time to create their online courses, is essentially saying that they don't have the time to do the very thing that is going to give them more time!

As soon as your content is online, you can immediately take on a potentially unlimited amounts of customers, without having to do any extra work! You can send customers to your self-study options instead of you needing to go to that coffee meeting, or jump on that skype call, or deliver that webinar. By putting your knowledge and expertise into an online course, you are eliminating the need to continue to put your time into personally serving your customers.

Still putting this at the bottom of your priority list?

Time Is Money

The very same argument is true for those who want to make more money, but can't because they don't have the time to take on any more customers.

I was on a coaching call with a client of mine, Jessica. She has contacted me because she really wanted to get a plan together for her online course on first time parenting. By 2 hours into our call, I had helped her get her complete online course plan written out, every module, lecture and learning outcome, ready to film! She could have had it live within a few days.

Then she hit me with a sentence that I've lost count of how many times I've heard, *'I'm not going to do my course yet because I'm really busy with other stuff and dont have the time right now'. '*

What other stuff?' I asked, knowing what was going to come next.

'Well I've got to earn money Sarah, and to do that I need to see my customers and with all of them that i need to see to earn my money, I don't have time for this just yet'.

I silently facepalmed myself and rolled my eyeballs with an unsurprised familiarity. I know full well that if you don't change anything, then nothing changes, and Jessica, like many edupreneurs was stuck in a self-imposed trap that quite simply was a never ending cycle. I knew she was never going to have time to create her courses (which would give her more time and money as a result) unless something gave way.

'Well why don't you drop one or two of your current customers this

week so that you can get this up and running by next week - which will then give you more time and money?' I asked. *'But I need the money they are paying me, I can't afford to drop them for a week to do this'.* Jessica exclaimed as if I'd just asked her to donate her head to medical research. Double face palm.

I'd love to say that this story had a happy ending, but I recently touched base with Jessica on Facebook and months later she still hasn't filmed her course, she's still cramming client advisory sessions into every waking hour she has so that she can get every cent from them until some epiphanous day magically presents to her more time and money (which obviously won't happen).

Sadly there are a lot of edupreneurs like Jessica out there. They keep pushing the very thing that they need to do to get more time and money aside, to keep doing what they are doing which clearly isn't where they want to be.

In 2016 I was in a training session with Rory Vaden who was teaching us that success is all about multiplying our time. He essentially put it to us that success is not related to the number of tasks we do in a day, but how we multiply the minutes in a day.

In a world where there is so much demanding our time and attention, my favourite thing he said was *'give yourself emotional permission to spend time on things today, that will give you more time tomorrow'*. As someone who is always 'busy', yet obsessed with insane productivity, this sentence really stood out for me.

If we go about our days thinking that we are 'spending'

(another way of saying 'giving away') each minute that we have, we can feel stressed, anxious and even guilty about how we spend those minutes, as once they are gone, they are gone. We are in a trap of literally exchanging our life for whatever we are doing in that moment, and if it does not equate to the value of our life in our minds, we start to experience dissatisfaction and unhappiness. BUT, when we see time as an investable resource - as something we can get back, then we can use it to our power. We can use it to multiply what we get back from each minute we put in.

If we spend more of our time focussing on tasks right now, that are going to ultimately give us more time in the future, then we have quite literally multiplied our time.

This could be spending time writing up detailed instructions and training videos for completing a task that we do regularly, so that we can start delegating that task from there onwards to an assistant or employee. It could be turning our services and knowledge into online courses so that we can divert our customers to the self-service options before booking up our time.

Yes, you're busy, but if you want more time tomorrow, you need to invest some of the minutes you have right now to get more back in the future. It's TIME to create your online course, right now. TICK TOCK TICK TOCK TICK TOCK……

If we spend more of our time FOCUSING on tasks right now, that are going to ultimately give us *more time in the **future***, then we have quite literally multiplied our time.

CHAPTER 12

What If Nobody Buys It?

The fear of rejection can stop so many of us from ever even attempting to go after our dreams. I've watched friends avoid asking someone they like to go out for dinner with them just incase their crush said 'no'.

I've heard hundreds of my past students and clients tell me that they don't want to 'risk' putting all of the work into their course just incase nobody buys it. I even saw one edupreneur post in a course creation Facebook group I am a member of, that she was thinking about unpublishing her brand new online course and deleting it altogether because she didn;t make a sale on her first launch day. Talk about putting pressure on yourself.

The thing about this mentally is that when you already have nothing, then you don't have anything to lose. If you don't try, you have 100% of nothing, if you do try, then you have a 100% chance of getting a result.

If my mate did ask the girl he liked to go for dinner, she 'could' have said yes. And if she said no, he would still be in precisely the same situation - having dinner on the couch with his cat.

If we create a course and nobody buys it, then we at least have a product to take to our market to get real feedback on as to why nobody is willing to exchange their money for it. Courses, indeed any product or service, needs continuous iteration. The world around us changes so rapidly, that if we don't forever evolve, adapt, develop and change our content, then they will eventually go out of date and shrivel up before us. You need to have something out there to start with.

Steve Jobs didn't just miraculously pop the Mac computer out of his bum-bum. Have you seen some of the monstrosities that came before it as it was being iterated and adapted to what the market really wanted?

Do your market research right in the first place and your mojo will have no excuses to go on a walkabout.

Market Testing is Your Ultimate Assurance

Market testing is critical to ensuring that you are about to invest your time wisely into creating a product that is going to be profitable.

This market research and testing phase is all about ensuring that you are building a product that your audience actively wants and needs right now.

At the most fundamental level, if there is market demand, then your course should sell. If it has market demand and your course doesn't sell, then you know it's a marketing issue that you need to address, not a problem with your course per se.

If you have followed the market testing steps outlined in my book 'Entrepreneur to Edupreneur', then this should not be a mojo-killer that affects you. However, even when you have done every aspect of market testing you can never ever predict the exact behaviours of the marketplace.

I once had a multimillion dollar contract delivering training under a Government funded scheme that had been federally set into place for the next 6 YEARS at minimum.

Only a few months into the contract, the federal budget for it got unexpectedly slashed overnight and i lost everything - even though it was in demand (as the users still needed my services) there was simply no money in my client's pockets to pay for it.

Similarly, you cannot predict what will be going on in the lives of your market at the time you launch, so you need to be sure that you have adequately assessed your market demand so that you can eliminate this from your 'root causes'. If you do have a flat launch, begin exploring what else needs iterating and simply try again with version 2.0.

Go back to your purpose and your 'why' again - this should give you a little motivation boost so that you do not feel like deleting your course like my friend in the Facebook group did.

Then ask yourself if you really have presented your course to the right target audience.

Too many people create a course, press publish and then present it to entirely the wrong people and wonder why it didn't sell.

You need to know exactly who your audience actually are so that you can laser target your offering to the people that actually need it.

If you did conduct thorough market research, and you really are doing all the marketing you can yet nobody is buying, then adjust your course, tweak your landing page, massage your written sales copy, adjust the price, do a special offer, and try again with version 3.0.

Find alternative ways of getting your content into people's hands - partnering, conferences, inside a book. People are nervous these days and may just need some other people that THEY trust to start saying great things about it.

Build an Audience Now

Finally, start building your audience now.

It is never too soon to start building a following of people who are seeking the information that you have - even if you haven't even started on your course yet.

Create a Facebook group that will attract your target audience, start writing blog posts that are in line with your course topic, set up an email database in something like MailChimp, ActiveCampaign, ClickFunnels or ConvertKit so that you can start building up an email list of people who are interested in your field of expertise. That way, when you do eventually go to market you have an instant group of people to test from and sell to.

Give yourself comfort in knowing that successful course creation and launching is not about getting it perfect first time. It's about creating something, anything, from which to base your first iteration upon until you do start getting results.

CHAPTER 13

What if People Steal or Copy my Ideas or IP?

Even with all of today's technology, we simply cannot fully protect our IP. If it goes online, it's going to get stolen, copied or accessed by people who haven't paid for it. Thats a fact.

Look at huge music artists and Hollywood producers - they have all of the iron fists and legal behind them to protect their content, yet I'd expect that most of us have watched a pirated movie or listened to a song that we haven't paid for before. If people really want to get their hands on your stuff the bad way, they will.

Although we cannot stop it happening altogether, we can do a few small things to reduce the chances of it happening or make it a little harder - we will cover these in this section.

Copy Cats Copy Cats

I'll never forget the first time I had my content copied.

A competitor of mine had quite literally copied my entire website word for word, and just as I was getting over that surprise, I realised that the same person had also copied my entire LinkedIn profile word for word as well! It was so bizarre that it was funny.

But fast-forwarding ahead to today and the very nature of my work - teaching people how to teach - means that I am actually the cause of almost all of my own copy-cats. Almost all of my competitors today were at one stage my students. Although I must admit I sometimes feel the odd pang of *'that's not fair, I worked so hard to build that from scratch and you just copy-pasted it'*, I have to look at their efforts to replicate me and my success as a credit to my excellence.

Nobody would want to copy me, if they didn't aspire to be me, look up to me and enjoyed thoroughly the training that they had from me.

I have Google Alerts set up to receive automatic email notifications whenever certain keywords are published online, and it never ceases to amaze me just how many of my articles get copied almost to the word. My course landing pages, curriculum, and even videos get copied to the word.

Does it bother me? Well, a little yes, but not to any great degree. You see, I remember my purpose, my why, my reason for doing everything I do. It's to educate people. As many people as possible. And one of the main reasons I choose to educate educators, is because i know that will help me be the catalyst to global education at an accelerated level.

If I teach one educator how to create their own courses, and they then go on to educate 100 people - I have ultimately been responsible for 101 people getting trained. With that in mind, if I ever find myself thinking 'that's not fair' at someone copying my content, I remind myself that my copycats are actually *helping* me on my mission. And if any of my copycat students go on to be a great success using everything they got from me - well, I make them my case study. We must ask ourselves, *'is it more important who gets the credit, or the fulfillment of the greater mission?'*.

All that aside, take this seriously too - know when it gets taken too far as there is a line. When your IP is being used against you in a competing manner, to the point that it is actually taking money out of your pocket, THEN you need to address the situation. I foolishly jumped head-first into an association with one of my past students who attended my Course Creation Bootcamp in late 2016.

In two days on my bootcamp, he created his first online course and made more than $20,000 USD from it in the following 4 weeks. We discussed him being a guest speaker on my future bootcamps to teach my students about the marketing techniques he applied to make such impressive sales. In the throes of excitement, a whole joint venture program had been planned within hours and we agreed that we'd do a bootcamp as a team, where i would continue to deliver my usual course creation training, online school set up, filming, film editing, email automations and edu-business planning and authority marketing training; and he would add a few days onto the end to teach them Facebook, Twitter and YouTube advertising. Each to their own area of expertise. It all sounded good to me.

Within hours of coming away from the conversation, I was sat on my sofa at home with my husband, scrolling through my Facebook newsfeed whilst the adverts were rolling on the TV. Suddenly my thumb hovered over a post that completely threw me. A complete stranger had posted one of my exact online course market research surveys and scripts that I give to all of my bootcamp students, with my new business associate tagged, thanking HIM for all of his help creating her online course for her...... I was gobsmacked. No part of our agreement was that he could teach my course creation content. No part of the agreement was that he could go off and start providing services to clients outside of our proposed bootcamp. I called him immediately and he brushed off the event as him trying to help generate interest and exposure for our upcoming joint bootcamp, he told me not to worry and enforced that I really ought to trust him if we are going to work together - he'd be putting 50% of the income into the shared 'pot' and that I should be thanking him, not accusing him of anything untoward. I spent most of the phone call with my jaw on the floor - there was nothing I could do, it was too late, he's already gone and done it behind my back.

If I've learned one thing it's this - if anyone says to you *'Don't you trust me?'* they should absolutely not be trusted. It's an extremely manipulative and passive-aggressive way of making *you* feel bad about *their* behaviour. Anyone who can comfortably blame others for their own behaviour via manipulative talk is the last person on earth you should ever trust. Run away. Fast.

Cut a long story short, our association came to an end only a few months later when I discovered (from his own social media posts) that he had gone on to provide course creation services to 13 clients behind my back, with my IP, without authorisation, using my name to score himself the business and did not share a cent of income with me. Im talking services that were advertised at $5,000 USD per client - which meant he had taken my IP whilst we were still in 'partnership', then used my name to deliver my services to the value of $65,000 USD. He then took all of my systems, content and IP and set up a competing course creation service. You couldn't make this up. Although I must take some responsibility for the fact that I made it so easy for my business content to get stolen, this type of behaviour is parasitic at the most extreme level and is when copy-catting goes over the line and things need to get serious, after all, it's blatant theft. When somebody uses your own content, IP and name to take money out of your business by illegally replicating or using your copyright material and IP, bring in the legals immediately.

I'm not going to lie at first I was angry *'The injustice of it all'* i heard myself angrily shouting in my head. *'It's so unfair that someone can just steal all of my years of hard work for their own gain!'* I sobbed alone in the shower.

But then I noticed something. I noticed that everyone else had noticed. He was not in anyway shy about sharing everything he was doing very publicly online.

I was inundated with messages from people stating how shocked they were to see this person so publicly and proudly steal from me (after he'd so publicly and proudly told the world that he'd learned it all from me only a few months before), and that his own actions had very clearly sent out a message to the world of the kind of person that he was.

I had established myself so strongly as an expert in my field, with YEARS of published content, clients, products, services, blogs, books, courses and more behind me in this space, that it was more than obvious to everyone watching that I was being copycatted.

The lesson in my story? Sharing your IP and content is

precisely what makes you an expert and establishes it as an evident fact that you are the leader in your space.

Only by sharing your knowledge, tips, expertise and videos can you attain and maintain that position. If you never put it out to the world for fear of somebody pinching it for themselves, then nobody will ever be helped and you'll never gain the position in the first place.

The best protection of your IP is the undeniable proof that it is YOURS, by testimony of people that it has helped, plenty of historically published evidence and a reputation of being the best in the business at what you do.

When you have this, the copycats can pinch, leach and scavenge all they like, because everyone will know that pinchers, leeches and scavengers are all that they are from the evidence that you created it first.

As mush as it can hurt, it really isn't the end of the world if it happens, and I go with the premise that I'd rather risk a few copycats and help millions of people, than hide it all away and help nobody.

I'm no IP lawyer, but here are a few simple and easy ways that you can protect your IP when you go out to the world with what you know:

Get Trademarked

If you really are concerned about the protection of your business, then it may be worth you considering getting a Trademark. It's not suitable for every business, it doesn't necessarily cover all IP, and it's not cheap either. However, I would recommend at least speaking with a Trademark Attorney and getting their opinion on what your options could be and what it would protect for you.

Post It

A simple tip I learned in the early years of my business when I was lacking in coin but had a lot of course content that I wanted to protect, was to quite simply print out your whole course, including the curriculum plan, lesson plans and content; then post it to yourself as tracked and recorded delivery, then never ever open it. If anyone ever reproduced your content and it went to court for dispute, you have the dated proof that your content came first and that they had in fact copied your IP. Simple, yet effective.

Time Stamp

Similarly when it comes to online content, don't forget that if you are sharing publicly, that is your proof that you published it first! Every blog post has a published date on it and so does every YouTube video, social media status and livestream. If a replica piece of content comes out after yours was published, it's glaringly obvious who got it from who.

Show Your Face

I host my online courses on marketplaces as well as my own LMS (Learning Management System), and these marketplaces are notorious for hackers downloading your content and re-selling it on the black market. Although I'd certainly report any instance where i found out someone was making money illegally from anyone else's content (all of the marketplaces have special customer support channels that focus on dealing with these issues), I can only see the bigger picture and ultimately THANK the pirates - because at the end of the day, they are conducting free marketing services for me.

The first way I protect my content is to make almost all of my training in 'talking head' video format - literally meaning that it is my face on the screen delivering the training. So regardless of who is watching it and how they obtained it, it is still me who is clearly being seen as the expert. It is still ME, my face, my words, my head, my name, that is being presented to the audience - which means that I am the only one who can get the credit for it, or any subsequent business from it.

Watermark

Ensure that that you name and/or website URL or watermark is shown in your training videos and documents. You have to be very careful about this, as each of the online course marketplaces have very different rules about what you can and cannot do in terms of branding and self-promotion;

but where you can do it, do. That way, if your content has been shared illegally (and the actual viewer may not even realise that they got it unfairly), if it has your logo, face and website on, it's still going to be you that gets the praise, credit, fans and subsequent business that may arise from someone watching that content. So as much as I don't want to encourage anyone ripping my marketplace content, i don't waste time getting too upset about it, as it's all doing me a favour in spreading my message and my exposure in the grand scheme of things.

Make it Common Knowledge

Have you ever seen those memes on social media, you know, the images with some generic, overused inspirational quote on them?

You read them and you KNOW that it was not written by the blogger who shared it (and had their own URL next to the quote). You know, without doubt the second you read it that it is someone else's words being used by another person to build their own following. I started a little saying in late 2015 'Courses are the new business cards', which later got hijacked by others and used as their own.

I even received a marketing email with my own quote as the subject heading but presented as the words of the sender. This got me wondering what all of these famous leaders think when they see their sayings written on memes and shared around the world. I bet they never think *'oh that's not fair, that's my word'*. I'd imagine they think something along the lines of *'i am so happy that i have made this impact that is now rippling to touch lives far further than i could have reached alone'*.

To make real, far-reaching and long lasting change, we have to allow others to assume ownership of our very message themselves.

To get a news story to go viral, the media has to get everyone talking about it. They have to get people to assume the argument as their own, or nobody would take the action to share it with others.

If you have a 'saying', an approach, a process or something you consider 'yours', don't ask yourself how you can wrap it up and protect it; find a way to make it so big and so 'you', that no matter where and how it is used, everybody knows that it is yours. Say it in every video, every blog, on your website, in your email signature, every interview you do and everywhere you can in the public eye. Make it undeniably yours, but allow it to 'belong' to whoever would like to identify themselves with it too - after all, this is how you build a tribe and precisely how and why I created 'Edupreneurs' and defined 'Edupreneurship'. I wanted to become the undeniable leader of something, but do so in a way that I could give away something for others to assume as their own - an identity that they could call theirs, but that ultimately will always come back to me as the leader of for birthing it in the first place.

Keep an Eye Out

Simply keep a little watch out on your stuff. I use Google Alerts, which is a completely free Google tool which allows you to enter in various search terms, such as your name and certain words and phrases that you use. Once set up, Google will email you whenever those words or phrases are published online - then you can check them out and see if you have been plagiarised, properly referenced or it's just a coincidence.

You can also use plagiarism checkers to see if your work has been duplicated anywhere. There are lots out there, but one of them is http://www.copyscape.com where you can insert the URL to your blog post for example, and it will then scan the web for matching content.

Have a Copyright Policy

I'm no copyright attorney, but you automatically assume copyright to the way you present something as soon as you write it. However, you can create your own policies that you can use to help guide and educate the public about what is ok and what is not. Although this won't necessarily protect you legally, it can help the breaching of your preferences simply because people will be better informed.

Firstly, consider including a copyright symbol or disclaimer on your content. Although it does not offer extra protection it can make people think before they reproduce it.

Secondly, write up a very clear list of what you deem as 'ok' when it comes to referencing you, using your content and sharing or reproducing it and what is not ok. Give them some guidelines as to the types of things they would need to ask your permission for and what they can do without having to ask for written permission.

Make it Truly Valuable for Only One

IP is often accessed 'naughtily' when people 'share' access they should exclusively have by sharing their login details with others.

However, when courses are highly interactive, have private exclusive facebook groups, discussion areas, one on one coaching elements, face to face training elements, live Q&A webinars and certificate issuance, it suddenly only becomes wholly valuable to one person, as the most valuable parts simply cannot be shared. This will never eliminate sharing, but including these un-shareables certainly reduces it.

If You Hold it Back, You Are The Thief

It can be easy to fall into defensive mode, to protect our intellectual assets and lock it all in an inaccessible knowledge dungeon where it's 'safe' from the lazy pinchers. I was once delivering one of my one-on-one course creation days with Krista, a client of mine who delivered business development training for the multi-level marketing industry.

As Krista and I sat down and started discussing which course topic she was going to go with, she said something that I've been hearing a lot more frequently of late. She said that she really really wanted to do her course around a specific list of business tips that she had compiled to help MLM businesses. *"But, I can't"*, she declared to me.

'What do you mean you can't?' I asked. *'Well because, there is this one woman who keeps on copying everything I do. Like, everything. So if I do this course I KNOW she's going to copy it, so I'm thinking of doing something else instead'.* I was mortified for her potential customers.

'So you are going to hold back all of your knowledge and stop all of your MILLIONS of potential customers from hearing it, JUST so that ONE person DOESN'T see it???' Can you see the madness in this?

We can become so obsessed with protecting ourselves, that we forget about those who we are trying to help by producing it in the first place.

What is is worse. One person copying you (which ultimately helps more people you are trying to help), or nobody ever getting your help?

Nobody Can Ever Be You

The most wonderful thing about being human is that we are all so different. People can copy our words, our writing, our ideas and our services, but they can never BE us. Thats one thing that nobody can ever take from us.

And here is the best part. People don't buy 'stuff', they buy people.

I could give you my exact scripts, my content, my slides, i could even give you my dress and underwear.

But put us side by side, doing the exact same thing in the exact same clothes, and some people will hate me and love you and vice versa. Because people like people. The way we speak, the way we look, the tone of our voice, how we hold our bodies, who we do or don't remind them of, how we make them feel in our non-verbal communication and much more of the subconscious subtleties that are really behind any buying decision we make.

I am very aware of the fact the despite my growing competition daily and the number of people that are now out there trying to take some of my market with my own content, they will never be *me* which means that they are never really going to be a threat.

CHAPTER 14

What If My Video's Are Not 'Hollywood' Perfect?

I have taken $5 courses on Udemy that were way better than ones that I've paid in excess of $25,000 for. Fact. And by 'better', I mean what I learned from them.

The $25,000+ courses I have taken had all the lights and bling; the private multi-million dollar mansion, the showy email campaigns, closed captioned videos, adrenaline-pumping intro music and big Facebook groups to boot. But almost every time, it's been the simple, homemade $5 courses that win my highest ratings.

This is because today, quality is not determined by how long a course is, whether it's been filmed by a professional crew over looking the most expensive suburb on earth, or how many effects have been used to animate the speakers on-screen name.

In a world saturated in information, 'quality' is often determined by the learners who feel that a course has given them the information they wanted, as quickly and directly as possible.

Yes, it's great if you can afford to buy yourself a home studio, or better yet, hire a professional film crew, but for many edupreneurs starting out this isn't an option and i would highly encourage you to not let the idea that you need a Hollywood production, be what stops you sharing your expertise with the world.

These days it is becoming more and more commonplace and accepted that freelancers and self-employed business owners work from home, usually in a spare room or a corner of the kitchen table. Remember that people are coming to you and your courses for the content, not to judge your backdrop.

If you are ashamed of your lounge room wallpaper, you could buy a cheap sheet of material to place behind you, or get a cheap banner with your business logo made and block off your surroundings that way.

If you don't have very good lighting and are worried that will affect your professionalism, then simply record 'voice over' slides or screencast videos. Your sound is important if you want to meet the quality criteria of online course marketplaces and enable your learners to actually be able to clearly hear what you are saying; but having a Hollywood production of a training video is certainly not a *necessary* requirement to help change people's lives.

No online course is stuck that way the first time it's published. Simply upgrade your content as you start bringing more money in and becoming more experienced.

There are a number of free tools and apps out there that enable you to create really professional looking videos from home, without the cost. In fact, my first home studio (which included two large soft box lights on stands and a backdrop in three colors with the stand) only set me back $256.

I made that back in the first 15 minutes of releasing my first online course.

Simply do a little learning on YouTube, or if you really want to get stuck in to course creation, take my online course on *'How To Create Profitable Courses'* and with a green sheet of material and some good lighting, you can easily produce studio quality training videos from your kitchen.

CHAPTER 15

What If People Criticise Me or Don't Like Me?

No matter how good we are, how nice we are, how hard we work or how much we give, there will ALWAYS be people that don't like us.

It's nothing personal, sometimes we click with people and sometimes we don't, often without any justifiable reason.

This happens a lot. Jealous people will do all they can to make themselves look better. Green eyed, scarcity-minded no-hopers will go as far as they can to bring you down to try to lift themselves up.

When people feel as though they do not have much to give, or at least, not as much as you have, the ONLY road they believe they have is yours - and that they can only drive on it if they run you off the road first.

Instead of getting angry at these people, I feel sorry for them. As an educator, I truly believe that everyone is a treasure trove of content, information, knowledge and expertise; and if they cannot see that or have the confidence to share it with their own unique voice, instead of trying to run them off the road in retaliation, we should try to find it in ourselves to offer them a lift. When they see your life from behind your windscreen, they may decide they don't want your road after all, and you might be able to show them that they have enough resources to build their own road in the process.

Generally speaking the only people who will poo-poo you will be these low self-esteem, self-doubting jealous kinds, your competition, and absolute nutters - all of whom we can either help, or simply not worry about too much.

But they will find ways to try to get under your skin, purely from the standpoint of trying to make themselves look or feel better in comparison to you.

If you charge less than they do for their products and services they will say that your content isn't good enough which is why it is 'cheap'.

If you price higher than them they will say you are scammy, money-grabbing, greedy and don't care about the 'poor' people.

If you have a special method for doing something, they will come up with 100 reasons why it's not the 'right' model.

They will mock words that you use or compare you to actual crooks to try to make you look bad; if they have 1 more day experience than you, they will say you are not experienced enough - and the list goes on.

The more ideas you have, the more room there is for people to disagree with you. The more people agree with you and love you, the more who will not simply by mathematical default. This can bring us new challenges in terms of trying to keep our self-esteem healthy and also in terms of managing our emotions enough to ensure that we make the right choices in the way that we respond to criticism or negativity that comes our way - but it is critical that 100% of the time that we go back to our brand before we so much a draw a breath.

Always Remember your Brand

When you receive criticism, judgement or are pulled into a negative, defamatory or 'risque' communication that is in the public eye (in fact even when it's secret as everything can end up online these days), never forget that the words you use and the WAY you come across, has far more impact on you than what anyone is saying. What people are saying is just their opinionated words and so are shallow in their weight. However *who you are being* is factual evidence of the type of person and business that you uphold.

Never respond like a kid in a playground - remember that you are a brand.

A friend and colleague of mine Dee Hutchinson, (who is also an INCREDIBLE leadership coach) and I were once having a conversation about a difficult situation I faced in business in line with this topic. She said *"believe people when they show themselves to you"*.

There is no greater proof of who somebody really is, than how they turn up and behave right in front of your own eyes. *"Try to imagine yourself as a huge international fortune 500 company and how you would respond if you were the CEO of that"*, she advised.

Then she made me do it.

This removed my initial emotion-fuelled response and instead made me think very carefully about the impacts my reaction would have.

If I was a Fortune 500 company, my reaction as the CEO would likely hit the international news. It would be on newsfeeds, tweeted countless times, discussed and analysed by strangers and the reputation of that business in the public eye would all come down to the way I delivered a response to the situation in question. In that situation a number of professionals would be consulted as to whether the proposed formal response was appropriate, matched the brand, aligned to the ethical, moral and value-based policies underpinning the business, and finally it would be checked and approved by your legal team too.

Although we are not all Fortune 500 companies, this is a process we should ALL be following, even as one-man-band home-based businesses, IF we want to ensure we have a brand reputation to be proud of.

You see, your reputation is not based on what your critics, trolls or competition are saying about you - it's actually not even based on what you do operationally; it's based on *who you are being* and the impression you leave when people *experience* you. The way you make people feel is far more important than what anyone else says about you. This is the essence of a brand.

It's about the footprint you are leaving on people's lives and the emotions you conjure when you appear in their virtual, physical or mental world.

If our course creation mojo is being thwarted by a fear of people disliking us, then first we must acknowledge that no matter how good we are, making everybody like us is an impossible feat, and secondly to consider what it actually is that can beseech likeability.

How To Increase Your Likeability as a Leading Educator in Your Field

Lets face it. We all like to be liked.

Despite the content and objective of this section, I can readily admit to caring far more than I should about whether people like me or not.

I love to be loved and even avoid conflict or saying what's really on my mind at times, just so that I don't make anyone dislike me. There have been times where I have even flushed tens of thousands of dollars down the proverbial pan in keeping unproductive and unrequired employees on board, or maintained damaging business partnerships for longer than I should have, just so that I didn't 'make them hate me'. I know right, how silly! It makes me cringe to write it, but it's true.

Going back to the conversation I was having with my friend Dee, one of the reasons why I was facing such a personal challenge with my situation is because I feared that the choice i knew i had to make would risk the loss of a friendship.

She pushed me deeper into what I will call the *'Fortune 500 CEO'* exercise….

She made me recite what my brand was about.

She made me say out loud what I stood for and what I didn't.

She made me say what my business and my brand meant to me.

She asked me why my business reputation was so

important to me.

Before I knew it, I found myself crying quite uncontrollably.

This surprised me. *"Why are you crying?"* she asked. Not from interrogation, but with that nurturing 'coaching tone' that was telling that a lesson was coming.

I exploded into a passionate tirade *"because I built this business on an empty stomach; I've built it alone and with those I loved doubting my abilities; because I've seen the darkness of many nights trying to make it work; I've battled a GFC, dragged it across the planet, felt the sting of loneliness and repeated failure, failed relationships, empty bank accounts and homelessness trying to bring it to life. Because I've climbed every hill, conquered every mountain and eventually changed thousands of peoples of lives. Because despite all of that, I still love every ounce of it and it's as important to me personally as the sun is to the earth. Because I have given EVERYTHING to nurture it and bring it to life with every second of my entire adult life so far".*

A silence filled the air as I allowed the tears to rumble down my chin.

She looked at me with a smile on her face that made me feel like I was being shown myself for the first time. *"So don't you think that's worth the discomfort of making someone a little mad at you?"* she asked. I didn't even need to answer that. Of course it was.

Although some people swear blind that they don't care whether people hate them or not, given the choice, most mentally stable people would choose to be liked rather than disliked if they could.

So in this section I am going to explore what the

difference is between those 'edupreneurs' who create truly loyal fans and those who get ostracised by the very community they are trying to engage, so that we can put the course creation mojo-crushing fears of people disliking us to one side for good.

So here it is - the simple fact is that people buy 'us' - not our products and services. People buy who we are BEING, not what we are DOING.

The secret to likeability is in the *way* we build our networks and in particular, HOW we make those people FEEL about *themselves* when we communicate with them (directly or indirectly).

There is a well known story about Jennie Jerome, who was Winston Churchill's mother. When she was asked about having dinner with two men (Gladstone and Disraeli), she said -

*"When I left the dining room after sitting next to Gladstone, I thought he was the cleverest man in England. But when I sat next to Disraeli I left feeling that **I** was the cleverest woman in England."*

Guess who won the hearts of the nation during this time?

As experts in our field, it is important for us to lead with authority. Afterall, weak leaders have a weak following and it will be hard for our learners to feel like they are in good hands if we do not lead with a degree of confidence and power.

However, **how** we make people feel when we are leading with authority is something we must pay very careful attention to if we wish to be an educational leader that is liked. For Edupreneurs, getting this balance right can be a real challenge, as the very reason the majority of our audience come to us, is because they are seeking skills and knowledge from us - but if we communicate that in a manner that makes our students feel ignorant, incompetent and of lesser significance than us, we immediately lose their business AND our reputation.

We have all modelled what 'leadership' is based on that which we have been directly exposed to, or been led like others. Unfortunately, this isn't always a good thing.

I don't know about you, but I can think of teachers, kids club leaders and bosses in my past who not only crushed every ounce of soul in my body, but also made me feel nothing but hatred, disgust and utter repulsion towards them. Can you? Would you call these people 'likeable leaders worth following?' Would you say that they helped you learn and grow? Unlikely.

As a real life example, I was once scrolling through Facebook and came across a public status of a stranger.

Their status was about how they were thinking of creating an online course - my absolute passion.

Naturally, I saw an opportunity to help and offered some advice for online course creation. What happened next was nothing short of shocking.

The response to my advice and freely given support was to be mocked, sworn at and abused, not just by the person who had written the status about creating a course, but by a number of her friends too.

Turns out this person had created online courses before

so totally knew what she was doing - on account of that, my advice was a bit like serving her up a big fat plate of lemons to suck on. **Awkward**.

However, do you think her aggressive response made me want to do business with her? To give my money to her? and importantly to be led by her?

About as much as I'd like to perform a lobotomy on myself.

Even worse than just losing just me as a customer, because her post was public, my commenting on it meant that it showed up in MY newsfeed for all of *my* thousands of friends and followers to see too.

Within minutes my inbox - as well as groups that I am a member of - were inundated with comments from my own connections who had seen this person's response, and let's just say that she did not win any likeability points that day.

Because people buy and like you for **who you are being**, not **what work you are doing**.

I tell this story because it is very important for us as leaders and educators and people who are aspiring to become *likeable* authorities in our industry that we must be very aware that **who we are being** is more important than **what** work we are doing.

Everytime we speak and communicate with others online we are building our brand.

Our brand is who we are.

Our brand is how people feel when they communicate with us.

If we want to become successful industry leaders, if we want to build a following of people that like us and buy from us consistently; if we want people to share our work, celebrate our successes and encourage others to follow us too, then we must be very aware of who we are being - because people by us, they don't buy what we sell.

Here are some of the key things that as educators, Edupreneurs and leaders, we must never forget if we would like to be successful, liked and even loved along the way:

1. Always Make New Friends

Success often does come down to who you know

Need a book launch to go well?

Want your blog post shared?

Want to build partnerships with people with huge lists?

Want to get connected to an influencer?

Whatever it is that you are looking for is much easier to obtain when you know someone, who knows someone. That's a fact.

The thing is, how can you expect people to do you any kind of favours, if they don't like you?

I have found in my 11 years in business, from my own

experiences trying to build my profile from nothing, and from many who have contacted me to ask for my help when they've just started out; I can categorically say that help is not handed to you based on how many people you know, or how many people are on your list, or how influential you are.

Help is handed to you based on whether you're a nice person or not.

Help his handed to you because you are genuine, kind, considerate, enthusiastic and clearly willing to help those individuals back if they ever needed a favour returned.

I see so many business owners and entrepreneurs who are using the excuse that they have no money, that they have no connections and that they have no list as the reason why they are not yet successful, or the reason why they are not yet putting 100% effort into achieving their dreams.

Time and time again I share my story of how going from homeless to having a 7 figure business within 18 months was no lucky strike for me. I had no money, I had no supporters, I had no investors, I didn't even have a mobile phone - let alone a phone number to call! Jeez, I didn't even have a HOME! Yet I managed to succeed and I put this purely down to the fact that **I was willing to build relationships with people.**

I was willing to bare my soul and make friends.

I was willing to be helpful and give my time, my friendship and put my hands to use.

The saying *'it's all about who you know'* is absolutely true. However please keep in mind that it does **not** mean how many 'high up and influential rich people you know'.

It means 'how many *relationships*' you have made regardless of their status.

2. When you give without expectation, rewards come back tenfold

We've all heard the saying that '*giving is receiving*' and this is very much true in the world of Edupreneurship. You don't have to have a lot to give, in order to gain a lot back.

You can share somebody's post, you can leave a positive comment, you can recommend them to someone seeking their products or services. You could give them one of your products or services, offer to help them run one of their future events - there are so many ways that you can give to others. When you offer unexpectedly without any expectation of reciprocation you will be amazed at how far this will stay in the memory of those that you helped.

Not only does it make you feel good. From my own experience, unexpected gifts come back to you especially in the form of love, gratitude and support which to me is the greatest gift of all. No money, position or status can possibly trump the feeling of being loved and liked by others.

3. Act Immediately

You are wasting time if you do not act immediately when opportunities present themselves to connect with, or meet new people.

For a lot of people, the thought of networking fills them with so much dread that they'd rather knock their own teeth out to see the dentist than go 'networking'.

As human beings anything that is new and unfamiliar generates fear inside us - it's a natural instinctive response to protect us from possible danger.

This is why when we are faced with meeting new people for the first time we can sometimes feel nervous, shy and embarrassed - because we don't want people to judge us, think little of us or dislike us. Whether we consciously realise it or not, our body releases chemicals to make us feel deterred by that situation.

However if we are limiting the relationships and friendships that we're building, we are directly limiting our success and our potential, so we must learn to push through this fear, discomfort and dislike of networking if we wish to gain formidable success.

4. Everything in Business is About People

People buy people, not products.

People follow people, not marketing copy.

People love people, not branding and services.

You can hide behind your emails and your beautifully designed website all you like, but if you stop building relationships your success will curl up and die.

Therefore grab every opportunity that presents itself to build a new relationship. You don't have to go 'all out' to meet up with someone for coffee. In fact, I'd go as far as saying be careful about how you are investing your time. Think wisely about how you build these relationships; a quick phone call, or a few messages in a chat thread can be enough to make a friendship start.

The only way to make those fear chemicals in our body subside is to show your body that there is nothing to fear - just new friends that you haven't made yet to go and meet.

5. People will want to help you when they feel emotionally connected to your mission

Share freely and passionately about what you care about and what you are trying to achieve.

I started my business working in the corporate space (business to business). My clients included the federal government, educational institutions and large industry bodies. I started my business at the wise old age of 19 years old and I was a blonde-headed female with a fresh-faced grin from ear to ear.

Naturally this meant that I didn't have that immediate heir of authority when I walked into large corporate boardrooms to present my training proposals. I felt like I had no choice but to be someone that I wasn't in order to 'survive' and 'prove that I could do it'.

It was stiflingly oppressive.

As I moved through the ebbs and flows of business sometimes high, sometimes low, I felt like I would lose my credibility if I did share any of the lows I went through. I was worried that I would look 'incompetent' if I dared share my entrepreneurial challenges and imperfect human nature.

I worked hard to conceal the cracks and silently suffered as I tried to paint a picture of perfection to the big wide world.

I didn't notice that as I filtered out all of my failings and only shared my wins and successes in the pure attempt to look 'professional' and 'good at my job', that I was actually slowly building a bigger and bigger wall of unapproachability.

The 'successes' that I thought was going to make people feel inspired, just made people feel like I was *'nothing like them'*, 'inhuman' - even intimidating and egotistical. I had no idea.

Then one day, I'd had a particularly bad day in business. The Government had unexpectedly retracted a budget that funded almost my entire client base and I lost *everything* overnight.

$2.7million in contracts, my office, 23 staff and gained a 6 figure tax debt that now couldn't be paid. It sucked.

Like most level-headed entrepreneurs, my immediate response to this situation was to have a deep and meaningful few weeks with a bottle of wine.

Eventually I ran out of self-pity and with nothing to lose, I decided to share with the world what was going on. I held nothing back.

I told the shameful, gut-wrenching, heart-breaking, credibility-destroying full story right there on Facebook. I don't know why I did, but I did.

The response blew my mind.

The messages of love and support came flooding in. Recognition, acknowledgement and celebration poured in all around me.

It quickly became apparent that my image of perfection and constant success made me look *so* different from everyone that was around me, that nobody could relate to me at all. Everyone just thought that my life was perfect and that therefore they could not aspire to be me.

Since sharing my royal stuff-ups and disasters, my

following has grown, my connection with others has increased dramatically, my friendships are endless and the media love having me as a guest - all because struggle is much easier for people to relate to than constant success.

People don't buy your success, people buy you.

To buy you, they need to know who you are; they need to know your story and they need to know that they are like you too.

One of the greatest components of all of our favourite movies and books is that the hero is the one that is most like us. If we could not relate to the hero then we would not be able to idolize them or aspire to be like them.

I have found that the more I share my story - the highs, the lows the bits in between; the more human I am.

Importantly, I found that it doesn't need to be a great story of some magnificent feat.

You don't have to have climbed Mount Everest with a goat on your back to be admired by others; you simply have to show that you are human.

LOVE, JOY, EXCITEMENT, FEAR, TREPIDATION…. All emotions help you connect with your audience - allow your audience to 'feel' you by sharing your journey as you go.

Don't be afraid to share your stories - the good, the bad and the ugly. It's the only way to get everyone cheering with you when the happy ending comes.

> **ACTIVITY:**
> 1. What is your story?
> 2. How did you get where you are?
> 3. What challenges have you been through or are you going through?

Do not feel fearful about sharing this with others.

People buy you - not what you do.

6. Dig The Well Before You Are Thirsty

This means creating friendships long before you need anything from them and they will be there for you when you do.

7. Always Be Generous

I live by this one as so many people have helped me when I've been down on my luck.

I started from scratch like most entrepreneurs and found myself starting from scratch a couple of times after - there is no way I would have any of what I do today if other people hadn't shown me such generosity.

I had complete strangers give me a sofa to sleep on, put food in my belly, give me an internet connection to use, even borrow a car.

The generosity shown by these people will never ever be

forgotten and when the time comes that they need a favour I would give them everything I have in return.

But this point isn't just about being generous to those who have helped you - this is about being generous day in, day out to people you don't even know, or for no particular reason other than that you have something to give.

I'm not selective about who I help - I give my advice freely to those who are long term unemployed and homeless and to multi billionaires.

Give give give give.

Giving makes recipients grateful, thankful, fond of you and also feel like they owe you one back; and you just never know how that reciprocation may unfold.

8. Generosity Is The Currency of Friend-Making

People only really have three things to say about you to others:

1. They like you
2. They dislike you
3. They don't know you

When you give to others, you are only giving them something to sing your praises about.

9. Give and Ask for Help

If you don't ask for it people cannot give it to you.

A fundamental human need is to feel like we have a purpose; and that often comes from giving, providing for and helping others.

You can actually create fans by asking for their help.

When people feel wanted and needed, they feel good.

You will be amazed how many people will want to help you if you ask them.

Never be afraid to ask for help, direction, advice and guidance - you'll be amazed at what can come back.

- Be the connector - if you know people that can benefit from connecting with someone else, introduce them to each other
- Use the 'Benjamin Franklin' method to your advantage - this is all about asking people for their advice or recommendation when you meet them.

For example, if you're going to a new town or location, reach out to someone and ask a recommendation for their favourite bar or restaurant. You never know, they may end up offering to show you around themselves.

> **ACTIVITY:**
>
> 1. Who are you who are you being?
> 2. Who do you want to be seen as?
> 3. What impression are you painting of the kind of person that you are?
> 4. Do you come across as a likeable, lovable, friendly, approachable person that others would like to be friends with?
> 5. Would you consider yourself the kind of friend that you'd like to have?
> 6. What can you do today to start being more likeable?
> 7. What can you do to build better relationships with others today?

So there we go.

Having likeability isn't some magical gift bestowed upon you by the 'friend fairy' at birth. It's not a secret formula or uncrackable code. Its simply thinking about who we want to be, and behaving in a way that is congruent with that.

Still worried about people not liking you?

It's time to shine.

Never forget that the words you use and the WAY you come across, has far more impact on you than what anyone is saying. What people are saying is just their opinionated words and so are shallow in their weight. However **who you are being is** factual evidence of the type of person and business that you uphold.

Your REPUTATION is not based on what your critics, trolls or competition are saying about you - it's actually not even based on WHAT YOU DO operationally; it's based on **who you are being** and the impression you leave when people experience you. The way you make people feel is far more important than what anyone else says about you. This is the essence of a brand.

*The secret to likeability is in the way we build our networks and in particular, HOW we make those people FEEL about **themselves** when we communicate with them*

You are wasting time if you do not ACT IMMEDIATELY when opportunities present themselves to connect with, or meet new people.

NEVER BE AFRAID to ask for help, direction, advice and guidance - you'll be amazed at what can come back.

CHAPTER 16

What If There Is Too Much Competition & I Can't Compete?

It's completely normal to feel a little threatened, envious and even slightly frustrated by your competition - they have more followers, they have better ideas, they have prettier landing pages, they have more content, bigger courses, nicer downloads, fancier video production than you.

Maybe they executed something before you did so now it will look like you are copying them if you follow through with what was an original idea you had and it infuriates you to no end that they are constantly in your way.

A little envy, frustration and internal challenge is healthy. It's good for you. It keeps you on your toes and keeps you improving. If you didn't have any competition then you wouldn't *need* to change and you'd go stale, dry and boring. In a world that is ever evolving, anyone or anything that doesn't change will eventually become extinct. If competition is a driver of innovation, development and positive iteration to a business or an industry, then in my eyes it's a very valuable and highly necessary part of our entrepreneurial existence.

Don't let your weeds grow while you admire their garden

So yes, checking out your competition and getting a twisty bit of envy in your guts is ok. In fact it's important to occasionally peak over the garden fence to see what they're up to - If you don't then you cannot ensure that your products and services are competitive or superior.

However, peek with caution. If you become overly preoccupied with what your competitor is up to, poking your head over and enviously looking at their beautiful garden to the point that you don't even notice that the weeds in your own patch are beginning to choke your land to death; or you are feeling overwhelming emotions about their every action - then you know that you have let it get too far.

Their successes are not your failures

It can be an all too common experience for us to focus so much on what other people are doing, that our thinking shifts to what we are NOT doing ourselves. We forget the massive project we are changing lives with on our side of the fence, and instead start obsessing about the fact that we haven't done 30,000 tweets this month like our competitor did.

We forget the client who we privately helped overcome a massive challenge yesterday, and instead beat ourselves up about the blog post we haven't written this month like our competitor did.

We forget about the questions we answered on social media that helped a whole bunch of users and instead give ourselves grief about the fact that we have not been publically bigged up in another Facebook thread by a raving fan like our competitor has.

You don't have to be losing for someone else to be winning. Focus on your wins, your successes and your triumphs.

You might not be envious if you knew the full story

A lot of people might be reading this and thinking, *"well how ironic Sarah, YOU are precisely the person who makes my insides twist up with envy"* - i know, many people have told me this. BUT they very rarely know the rough, the hard and the raw that went into getting the thing they are jealous about - and believe me, they wouldn't be jealous at all IF they knew!!

But in saying this, as someone that others now look up to as successful, i can assure you that I am never complacent. I know we are only as good as our last job, I know that business is no longer about the *big*, but the *fast*. I know that I can be overthrown at any minute and I know that I am in an industry where the competition triples daily.

There is no such thing as just 'getting there' - that's only the start. Once you are 'there' you have a whole other battle on your hands to actually stay there. So trust me when i say, I too am not exempt from the occasional feelings of inadequacy, nor the pang of jealousy when people have something that I want, or feel the fear when a competitor does something spectacularly epic that makes me feel like a loser in comparison. I'd go as far to say that if you didn't occasionally get these feelings, then you either don't care enough or are dangerously in the realms of complacency.

However, often the biggest problem is NOT the competition at all. Its US. It's the pressure that we put on ourselves and our confidence in our offerings.

If we truly ARE doing all that we can, then envy is less likely to creep in because we know we are operating at our best.

Competition is GOOD for you. It keeps you fresh, evolving and growing. But remember when you feel those niggles of jealously, that their life might not be as perfectly rosy as you imagine behind the scenes, or how hard they may have worked to get what they have.

It's about speed not size.

When I first started out in business my competition was an international multi-billion dollar organisation and the national government. Although I have to admit that my naivety about business at the wise old age of 19, coupled with a yet undamaged business enthusiasm was probably the biggest reason why I never quit at the starting line.

If I had seen the size of my competition as a reason why I shouldn't try, then tens of thousands of people today would not have been educated.

There is a perception that we have to be big, rich and famous in order to be successful or to make a difference. But this is so untrue.

In the not so distant old days of doing business the most successful companies were the largest companies. The ones with the most money and the biggest advertising budgets. The ones that could shout the loudest, afford the biggest billboards and dump the average person's annual salary on Facebook advertising.

In the old days of doing business it was a game of David

and Goliath and it was difficult for the small business owner, solopreneur or 'work from home' entrepreneur to even try to compete, certainly to even consider dominating a marketplace.

However business today could not be more different.

With freely available platforms to access millions of people every single day in multiple mediums, now anyone can compete.

Today's business success is not about size or budgets; it's about our ability to quickly and rapidly respond to our audiences needs and questions.

It's about he who is able to be the solution to a customer's problem the fastest and in the most personable manner.

The consumer no longer responds to fancy adverts or Hollywood production television advertising in the same way they did. Now significant business can be obtained by simply being available quickly and responding to questions as they're being asked.

It's also about rapid adaptability and flexibility to an ever changing market need.

The world is constantly changing and evolving and the bigger companies have heavier baggage to carry which drags them backwards and makes their change very slow. Larger companies have bureaucracy barriers and communication processes that halt relationship building and information delivery to the customer base.

However as a small business owner or solopreneur you are able to quickly respond and adapt to your market needs. You can quickly respond to queries and enquiries and you can do so in a very personable way.

Using apps such as the Facebook Messenger voice recorder you can leave personal voice messages in people's Facebook inboxes, and my personal favourite technique is to reply to emails with a personal video to every customer where appropriate. The responses I get to both of these methods of customer communication are overwhelmingly positive. People love the personal touch and when that extends to being able to hear your voice and see your face instead of just read words on an email, relationships develop much faster, as does the subsequent trust and business.

The next time you are feeling overwhelmed or disheartened at feeling as though you cannot compete with your larger industry players, remember that today's playing field is an even one and that you have significantly more advantages over the big guys than you think.

Know Your Unfair Advantages

I am in an industry where my competition increases every single day. I get served at least 3 different Facebook adverts daily of people offering course creation courses or services - many of whom are ex-students of mine too!

In a world where targeting is becoming more and more intelligent and we get to see real-time 'in your face' reports of what our competition are up to, how 'well' they are doing and what they 'apparently' have over us, we live forever at risk of falling victim to comparing ourselves to their accolades instead of celebrating our own.

One day, just as I had given birth to my first child and already feeling the fear that my newfound motherhood would make me fall into the shadows in my field, one of my biggest competitors released what can only be described as the most epic of course launches that directly competed with my *'HowTo Create Profitable Courses'* course. It was clearly sensationally planned, had had thousands of dollars ploughed into it, it looked like a million dollars, had an army of affiliates screaming about it from the craters of the moon and immediately got more likes and shares than I've drawn breaths in my life. I was absolutely ker-plunked and insanely jealous. With a newborn baby in my arms and new mum hormones raging through every cell in my body, I broke down into tears and proceeded to exclaim to my husband that I was doomed forever and might as well just give up on it all.

It can be so easy to feel like this when we allow our admiration or obsession with our competitors advantages, drown out our own.

This is when we must call upon the mirror and reflect heavily upon all of the advantages that we have; especially what I like to call our 'unfair advantages'.

List All of Your 'Unfair Advantages'.

Instead of focussing on all of the things that *they* have got that you have not and the things that they have done that you haven't done - think about all of the things that you DO have, that your competitor doesn't have and use these as your advantages.

In a world where my competition increases daily, because so many marketers are seeing the online learning industry booming billions of dollars, so many unscrupulous people are using it as a cash cow.

One of my competitors reached out to me in early 2017 to thank me for being such an inspiration to him and asked if there was a way that we could collaborate - which it quickly turned out was short for him wanting me to interview him on my podcast so that I could put him in front of my hard earned audience so that he could promote his competing services that he learned from me in the first place.

I tried not to laugh too hard and instead humoured him with a genuine attempt to find a mutually beneficial gap. Our conversation led onto whether or not he is qualified in curriculum design. His EXACT word for word response was this '*No. But I'll tell them I am*'. I swear black and blue, this person believed that this is an ethical way to conduct business.

I share this with you for two reasons:

1. You MUST be absolutely, completely and honestly truthful about your accomplishments and expertise. The world WILL find out the truth. It wouldn't take much for a client of that person's to say 'Show me your degree certificate then' **insert an explosion of his career - not because he isn't qualified, but because he lied that he is**

2. If you find out that you have something your competitor doesn't have, use it to prove that you are better. Even if this guy does go out and get a Degree in Education just to be on the same level as me, he's still always going to be years behind me in qualified expertise.

With this in mind, i know that using my qualifications and extensive decade-plus experience in my field is an extremely powerful advantage that I have over the newbies in my industry trying to slice a profitable pie while it's sexy.

I'm not arguing about whether 'qualified' actually does mean better or not - thats for the consumer to decide. But I can be sure on betting that it's an advantage that will favour me, and that lying about your credibility is a sure fire way to immediately lose any position you have in a market when they find out that you're not. BOOM, my unfair advantage over my competition.

ACTIVITY: Finding Your Unfair Advantage

Take a trip down memory lane and revisit every single one of your achievements, victories and successes. This is not time for modesty. This is time to get serious about all of the good that you bring.

Draw up a timeline of your life and list all of the positives you can think of at every stage of your life that prove you have what it takes to deliver the best online course in this topic; and as you are going through every part of your personal and professional history, list down all of your advantages and strengths on your very own 'boasting board' that you can draw from in all of your market, bios, profiles and 'about me' sections that exist.

Things that could count as unfair advantages over your competition:

- Formal training
- Qualifications
- Informal training
- Years of experience in the field
- Formal job roles in the field
- Informal work experience
- Charity work
- Awards
- Books
- eBooks
- Anywhere you have been published - contributing author, blogs, magazines, industry publications
- Interviews you have been on
- Podcasts you have appeared on
- Events you have run or been part of
- Conferences you have spoken at
- Challenges you have overcome
- An inspirational back story that you have
- Clients you have worked with - especially any big names
- Testimonials you have

Be different and the competition are gone

Don't try to bes AS good as them. Be different, better and even more expensive.

As soon as you are different, you are no longer competing. It is no longer an apple and an apple trying to push each other off of the branch - it's an apple and something else on totally different trees.

They might be able to outspend you, but they can never out-kind you

I remember when I just started out in the public arena and I looked up all of the big influencers in my field and was immediately intimidated by the enviable number of followers they all had, the big flashy ads they had and the ten gazillion 'likes' everything they published seemed to get.

I couldn't even get my mum to figure out how to like my page.

My inner imposter began listing out million reasons why I couldn't compete with these guys; they have a cataclysmically bigger marketing budget than me, they are more well known than me, they have more friends than me, they have more stuff than me, they have more affiliates than me, they have more influencer friends to partner with than me.

I was already thinking of quitting before i'd even started.

Before I gave myself a hernia, I sat down in my garden with a piece of paper and I said to myself, *'Right Sarah, you're right. We cannot outspend these guys with our measly marketing budget, and nor are we going to mess up our future ads targeting or moral compass by paying 3,000 rapid fingered workers in Kazakhstan to be my virtual friends for the sake of 'social proof'. However, I've gotta have something these guys don't have".*

Deep in thought with myself, my eyes wandered around my garden and stopped on a steaming pile of dog poop recently deposited by my hound, Molly. *"That's it!"* I realised. *"I give a sh*t!"*

I squeezed my dog and ran excitedly back into my office. I pulled a massive yellow ring binder off of my shelf, brushed the dust to one side and read through the 200+ feedback forms that were neatly bound inside. I flicked through the pages...

"You've changed my life Sarah",

"Thank you for all of your help Sarah",

"You are the kindest, most giving teacher I've ever had Sarah".

I pulled 4 more ring binders off of the shelves and kept reading..

"Nobody has ever cared like you do";

"My life will never be the same again because of the dedication you have for everyone you teach".

I ran to my computer, now with tears in my eyes, I opened the 'testimonials' email folder in my archive:

"You have no idea how much you have helped me".

"If everyone cared as much as you do about your learners outcomes, the world would be a very different place"......

Now sobbing big sploshy tears all over my keyboard, I realised that up until today, every success I had, had not come from having an ad budget, or money to throw at social media builders, or having flashy ads. I realised that everything I'd built and all of my successes to date had come from giving a cr*p about my customers, deeply caring about their outcomes, and by being a plain and simple helpful, kind and generous person. That was it. That's ALL I needed to keep doing.

"They might be able to outspend me" I said defiantly to the dog. *"But they sure as hell can't out-kind me. And I'll tell you what Molly - they can't out-work me either"*.

And that was that.

I set my mission back onto 'kindness cruise control' and I stayed on the road day in and day out helping, giving, sharing, caring and building.

After 18 months of never once taking my butt out of the drivers seat, I finally started receiving messages of thanks, love, appreciation, respect, and.... business. Lots of it.

"Sarah I've been following you for almost two years and I have learned SO much from you. You are so helpful and generous, an inspiration in a tough business world. I don't care how much you cost, I KNOW you are the one I want to work with - you've already given me way more value than whatever your price is".

We now live in a world where size and budgets, although helpful, are not at all *necessary* to attain success - financial, impact, reach - however you may define that. Today's secret to success is about being flexible, adaptable, 'real', accessible, friendly, kind and hardworking. Customers are choosing service providers, coaches and consultants who they feel connected with, even a level of 'friendship' with, rather than the ones who have the most followers or the sparkliest sales funnels.

If your mojo is feeling a little crushed by the size of your supposed 'competition' - remember that regardless of what they have, they cannot out-work, out-help or out-kind you; and that is precisely all you need to do to get anywhere worth being in today's world.

Success is not rooted in budgets anymore, it flows from flexibility and brilliance.

It's not only possible for you to compete, but to entirely dominate a marketplace with no more than that.

You can't work with 100% of the market

When it comes to competition, many of us behave as though there is only one customer left in the world and that it's a matter of life or death who gets them **waves an admission finger in the air**- I've been there.

The reality is, with 7.2 billion people on earth, there are more customers than any of us could ever ever service in our lifetime, regardless of the volume of our resources. And secondly, even if you *could*, it doesn't mean you'd *want* to service them all.

I mentioned earlier in this book that I'm not selective about who I help when i publicly share my information online - BUT, I am very selective about who I work with as this is when I'm giving my life to another person. In my opinion it would be wrong to myself, my staff, my family and definitely my customer if we weren't the perfect match for one another.

As time has gone on and my services have increased in demand, I've gone from literally accepting any customer willing to give me their money to now turning away more customers than I take on. Not because I've got 'stuck up' in anyway, but because experience has now shown me in its sharpest form, how important it is to only work with people who fit your style, processes and personality.

We often spend more time at work - with our customers - than we do with our own families, so why fill that precious time working with people that frustrate, irritate, exhaust and trouble us?

I've created a few systems in my business to 'litmus test' each customer that requests to work with me or my team, and if they don't fit the bill, they are someone else's customer, not mine. Enjoying my job - my life - and having a mutually appreciative relationship with my customers is far more important to me than earning money.

Who are you exchanging your life for?

> **ACTIVITY: Who are you exchanging your life for?**
>
> - What kind of customer do you want to work with?
> - Who is your 'ideal' client?
> - What kind of attitudes and outlooks do they have?
> - How do they behave?
> - What do they value?
> - What kind of person are they?
> - How involved in the process do you like to be?
> - Are you a 'hand-holder' or 'hands-off' provider?

If you can see how you are literally exchanging your life for people, you can start to see how important it is to realise that not everyone is your customer and that when you start to become more selective, you start to get more of the jobs that you love and less of the ones that you don't.

The best business comes from referrals - when people who had a great experience with you then go and tell other people about that experience. Since we all attract and hang out with people who are similar to us, it's highly likely that a great customer will only be friends with people who are equally great to work with - and so your world begins to change.

Don't ever be afraid to turn customers away. You might lose the odd bit of cash flow here and there, BUT, you'll gain freedom where you may have had frustration and anxiety caused by working with people who you just don't 'fit' with.

Ways that you can 'litmus test' your customers

Once you know *who* your ideal customers are, the next stage is to then find ways of filtering all of your enquiries so that you only let the perfect ones through.

Here are some methods I use in my enquiry, quoting and onboarding process to make sure each stage of my business services funnel is an opportunity to identify a mis-matched customer before work commences, to save us both any frustration or bad experiences:

- Require all enquires to come through a formal form on our website. If they can't be bothered to fill that in, we are not going to be a fit (see www.sarahcordiner.com/services to have a look)

- Have a specific list of services and require them to select from an electronic form precisely which services they want. If they can't find a service that's on the menu, we are not the right provider

- Have an electronic booking system for 'quick chats' or 'strategy calls'. If they consider themselves too important to book a call or wait for the next available slot like everyone else, we are not going to be a fit.

- If in that strategy call their personality or requests do not sit well (and a 'gut feeling' is an entirely acceptable indicator), then I explain to them that I am not the right provider for them. I use 'www.youcanbook.me' to do this and you can check out what my calendar looks like here: www.sarahcordiner.com/booking

- Send formal quotes from our accounting system instead of a written price in an email. This shows we are a serious company, have formal processes, that we will follow them up and that to accept the quote they have to press the electronic 'accept' button so that we have a legal record of what they accepted. If they don't like the formality of this, we are not a good fit.

- They must sign - with a real pen - a formal terms of service agreement which outlines explicitly what we have promised to deliver to them in clearly defined deliverables and what they must promise in return. You'll be amazed how many get all the way to this stage and then get huffy about having to 'go to the trouble' of a simple signature. On the very day I wrote this page I fired a customer who just found this request too much. No signature, no fit.

- Full payment for any service must be made before work commences. If you have got to this stage, and do not trust us to provide you the services as outlined in the signed agreement, then we are not a good fit.

- When payment is received, an electronic form must be completed by the customer with the information we require from them to complete their project instead of a chaotic and disorganised stream of emails containing various files and information. If they can't be bothered to follow our processes and complete a simple form for us to do our best work for them, then they will get a full refund immediately, as we are not going to be a good fit.

- Part of our services agreement covers termination and what happens if either party wants to pull out of the agreement. If at any point in the process of working with somebody, we feel that a client is not the right fit, we follow the processes agreed to to ensure they are not left with any losses, issue any owed refunds for work not yet completed and separate.

Maybe this gives you some ideas as to how you can take more control in your business, which will lift your confidence and that mojo!

There are MORE than enough customers out there, and you definitely do not want to work with them all.

Collaboration, not competition

When I first rocked up in Australia with no clients, I knew that I needed to quickly get in front of my target audience. And that one of the most rapid ways to do that was to find people that already had my audience in front of them.

But I couldn't just waltz up to people and say *'hey, I know you've probably worked your butt off for years to build this audience of people, but can I have them?*. No. I had to make it well worth their while to let me get in front of their most valuable asset.

I was offering was offering my workforce planning and development services and wanted to get in front of corporates who had 500+ employees who needed big workforce plans and career progression pathways developed, as well as training delivered to fill the identified gaps - one of MainTraining's major services still to this day.

I also needed to find these kinds of companies who were already open to training and consultancy from external providers. Not too much to ask, right?

What better way to get in front of these people, than via training providers who are already servicing them, have good relationships with them and trust them?

But here's the catch. How do you persuade your direct competitor, to happily and willingly introduce you to their best clients, so that you can essentially offer them directly competing services?

Well, I found a way to make it more than worth their while. I first figured out what they needed, what they most craved and desired - customers and money - and then I found a way to give it to them, so that I got a slice too.

At the time there was a federal fund available to businesses that would cover the cost of accredited staff training - (i was only delivering non-accredited training at the time). I read the guidelines inside out.

After a few days, I knew the entire 57 page Government

document back to front and inside out, and could even quote the criteria for application and reporting by the index codes.

I then reached out to the registered training organisations who specialised in delivering the accredited training that I knew my target customers would be most likely to want, and I asked them if they would like me to obtain the funding for their clients for them.

The training providers would have their training fully paid for and their customer would be delighted at having got the majority of the costs funded under the Government scheme, making them look amazing in the customer's eyes.

What did I get? 5% of the total project value as a brokerage fee that they would only have to pay me after the funding had been approved.

I quite literally had my arms bitten off with acceptances by the training providers and organisations alike. Within weeks I had secured over $3 million in funding for training for thousands of Australian workers, the training providers who introduced me to their clients got paid handsomely for some major accredited training projects; their clients got thousands of qualified staff for a fraction of the usual costs, and I had a 6 figure business with weeks of registering my company.

The training providers subsequently became my customers when they found out I also provided curriculum design and course content writing services and the corporates became my clients for further workforce development services and the soft-skills training that their existing providers did not provide. Literally everyone was a winner in a situation where we normally would have been 'competing'.

Your competitors really can become your best business partners - and even your clients.

I recently heard a term for this that I quite liked, 'co-opertition' - competition with whom we can work cooperatively with. Has a nice ring to it, doesn't it?

My whole point here is that one of the best ways to eliminate your competition, is to make them your partners. Make them *need* you.

Two businesses can do far more than one.

We all have different skill sets, strengths, preferences, resources and reach. You can double your reach, impact, workload, delivery and market share just by teaming up with one more person.

> **ACTIVITY: Finding Your Coopertition**
>
> 1. List out your top 10 competitors
> 2. List their gaps and weaknesses
> 3. List all of the ways that you can fill those gaps or complement their weaknesses
> 4. List their greatest wants and needs
> 5. Outline how you can help them get more of what they want and need
> 6. List your own greatest wants and needs
> 7. Outline how they could help you get more of what you want and need
> 8. List 5 suggestions of ways that you could work together to help eachother get more of what you both want and need

They are on the same journey

Your competitor may not do things the way you do, may have different values and ethics than you and prefer to do very different things at the weekend than you do, but in so many ways, they are exactly the same as you. They have bills to pay like you and are probably as worried about you as you are about them.

Business is tough and lonely sometimes. We all have the same stresses similar insecurities caused by self-employment and hungry mouths to feed around us - whether that is family, staff or both.

Sometimes we need to remind ourselves that all our competitor is doing is trying their best to survive and thrive, just like we are.

If they are in your industry, doing similar work to you, then you probably have a huge amount in common. Your passions, interests, expertise, goals, visions, aspirations, dreams and more. Instead of driving each other off of the road, see that there is enough space for both of you to cruise along comfortably on the road to a shared destination. If you can't handle that, then simply pick another route, there's got to be more than one way to that place.

Take your preferred lollies from the pick-and-mix pot, and leave the ones you don't like so that they can feed their families too.

There is enough to go around

Finally, when it comes to overcoming the fear of the competition, remember that there is more than enough business out there.

To receive abundance, you need to keep yourself out of the grip of scarcity.

ACTIVITY: There's Enough To Go Around

1. Write down exactly how many customers you genuinely have the capability and capacity take on right now, with the resources that you have.
2. Times that by ten. That's 10 times more than you could handle right now. What number is that?
3. Does that come anywhere close to the number of people available in your global marketplace?

No matter how niche you are, and how specialised your market is, I'm pretty confident that you could never handle it all. So let's stop worrying about there not being enough, shall we?

*Today's business success is not about size or budgets; it's about our ability to **quickly** and **rapidly** RESPOND to our audiences needs and questions.*

CHAPTER 17

What If They Think I'm Boring?

Content beats charisma.

I actually know a (not very nice) online marketer, who is rude, constantly swears online and is publicly aggressive. Yet surprisingly people like him.

This is because firstly, he shares content that the people who follow him find useful.

Secondly, he knows that there is a group of people who find his behaviour, attitude and personality 'funny' and 'interesting', and they do.

We must remember that the fact we are all different is a great thing when it comes to business, because we attract what we are attracted to and it's as simple as that.

All you need to do is attract the type of people that are like YOU, which means the only thing you need to do is just be you.

If you are going to find the people that resonate with you and your style, that's all you have to show them.

The key to connection is authenticity, and the only way to do that is to be entirely yourself.

I like to work with people like me, so if I tried to be someone else I would attract people who are not like me; and then I'd have an audience that I just don't gel with and that is not good at all.

You cannot ever be likeable to *everyone*, so don't try to be. Just be you, and you'll find more people like you too. There's nothing better than that.

CHAPTER 18

What If I Have Too Much Content?

Most edupreneurs and course creators that i work with don't have the problem of not having enough content; usually they have too much.

They come to me with a list as long as Rapunzel's hair of online course ideas and a laptop case full of hard drives with 'content', research and information on them that could be included.

One of the biggest problems that we have to solve is not what needs to be added to our courses, but actually what needs to be taken out.

What to do when you have too much content:

1. Go back to your learning outcomes - if the piece of information you are questioning does not directly help the learner obtain the learning outcome, then leave it out. This is about separating the 'need to know' and 'nice to know'.

2. Focus on the learner and how their life will be different by the end of the course - what will they be able to do, know and feel by the end of it?

3. Break it down into its smallest parts. The brain can only process so much at a time. Rather counter intuitively, the smaller the course is, the more effective it is and the higher the completion rates are going to be. As givers, we need to know when we are being over-generous to the detriment of the learners knowledge acquisition and to our own bottom line.

4. Decide whether your program will be better from a learning experience perspective - and commercially - if you made multiple mini courses instead of one huge course. You can still make it the same price (eg 10 x $10 courses instead of 1 x $100 course). This will also open up a market that may not have initially entered at the $100 mark, as well as provides more options from a pricing perspective.

   Eg, with 10 courses you could now offer a subscription model, or a payment plan, or drip release your content over a 10 week period, helping your learners implement in stages for the purpose of helping them get the results they are after. It also makes it more manageable for you to produce as the smaller parts reduce the overwhelm.

5. Create an 'appendices' or 'bonus' section in each course that houses all of the content that goes above and beyond the basic delivery of the learning outcomes. That way you are providing additional value in the form of further reading without overloading and overwhelming your learners

6. Cut the text down. Replacing your long form text files into checklists, bullet point lists and simple cheat sheets will be far more useful and consumable to your learners. By all means keep the long form in the appendices section, but

remember that all people want is the answer in its most direct form.

Don't feel like you have to cram an entire lifetime worth of knowledge and expertise into one course - save some for other courses too.

Create folders in a Google Drive, or Trello boards that are dedicated to housing content ideas for future courses. That way you won't feel like you're taking anything away from your learners, and you'll be starting to build out other courses at the same time!

CHAPTER 19

I'm Overwhelmed By How Much There Is To Do

When we see a beautiful painting, it is difficult to image how many miniscule steps and stages were involved in creating it. All we see is the end result and assume that the artist sat down and with the flick of a brush, it was done.

Similarly, many online course creators think that they have to paint a Picasso from the first stroke and then feel complete overwhelm when each stroke uncovers yet another skill that they don't have, or another piece of content that they could include, or a new piece of technology to learn and indeed, even a whole new language that they need to master too.

This sounds like the simplest advice ever, but I still get overwhelmed at big new tasks as I focus so much on the finished piece that getting there seems almost impossible. I have to remind myself to break every single tiny stage down into micro steps; into easy, manageable, achievable little actions.

I created an activity years ago when I was teaching goal setting to illustrate the power of breaking up a big task into the smallest parts. I call it the 'Draw a Dragon Technique'.

You can watch a video to do this exercise on my YouTube channel, but quite simply, imagine that I told a room of people to draw a dragon. That's it. No instructions, just an outcome to achieve.

Why not play along now? I'd like you to grab a piece of paper and draw yourself a dragon.

Done that? Everytime i start this activity in a training session, I excitedly observe what happens.

Some people look at me like I'm ridiculous

Some ask for more instructions

Some get angry at me for asking them to do art when they are not an artist

Some try really hard and get excited by the challenge

Some get distressed and upset that their picture isn't perfect

Some get their phones out and try to copy other dragon pictures

Some just sit there with their arms folded and do absolutely nothing

It truly is fascinating what I see every time.

The next thing I notice, obviously, is that everyone's dragons come out looking completely different. Some have angry dragons, some are happy, some are cartoon like, some have gone for a realistic approach, some have done facial close ups and others have included the entire dragon body and some look like a spider got drunk, fell in an inkwell and ran around on their page.

At this stage there is an interesting vibe of mixed emotions hanging around in the air.

This is because I set them a task without giving any regard to their existing (or non-existent) artistic abilities. I also gave them no road map as to how to get there, where the major milestones are or what signposts to look for to know they were travelling along the right route. I also gave them no clearly defined set of instructions as to precisely what the finished piece needed to look like.

With that in mind, it's pretty obvious why we get a room full of more frustration, distress and strife, than of driven, focussed results.

So we move onto the next stage.

This is when i give everyone a new piece of paper and ask them to follow me one line at a time.

I cannot be assured that everyone in the room is a natural artist, nor do I have time to train them to be. However, I know that I can teach them how to draw a straight line. And once I've taught them that, I know I can teach them to put 3 together to make a triangle.

Line by line and triangle by triangle, everyone in the room ends up with a picture of a dragon that all look very similar to each other.

I ask the room how that exercise felt. The solid response every time is a resounding 'easy'. *'So simple my kid could do that, and i could show them how'*.

The mood in the room is palpably different. I look at the group who are admiring their pictures proudly, quite surprised at how something so easy could produce a result that was far better than the first attempt they made.

Now here's the lesson from this exercise.

If we go straight to a blank page and try to jump straight to the end result, we will suffer immediate overwhelm. The journey isn't clear, our brain cannot fathom how it will get there and we go into displaying numerous types of 'avoid this' behaviours.

It is quite impossible to jump from starting to write a book, to having a whole book complete, without having to write it one letter at a time.

We need to break down our goal or task into its equivalent of little lines, tiny triangles and individual letters of the alphabet so that we can train our brain to not see the entire novel that needs writing, but simply just the next letter.

Break everything down into its smallest part so that it becomes a step by step journey.

For example, writing on your to-do list: "Build my online school", you will go straight to overwhelm, where does your brain begin?

Instead write a detailed roadmap that breaks down every step, eg:

1. Pick a platform
2. Sign up and create my account
3. Watch the training videos
4. Add my logo to the site
5. Select my site brand colours
6. Connect my PayPal and Stripe
7. Add a link to my social media profiles
8. Upload a photo of myself in the instructor section

By the way, this is not a full list of what needs to be done to set up an online school - it's just an example of breaking a big task down. But can you see how each of these things now make the task seem much more doable and manageable?

> ### ACTIVITY: Create Your Road Map
>
> Another thing that cause overwhelm is to see a really big to-do list.
>
> This is why i like to draw out a journey or a map instead of a massive long list that will just make me feel like I'm in a race that I can never win.
>
> I like to get post-it notes to begin with and braindump every task I can think if, then stick them up on the wall in order of what needs to be done first from left to right - a simplified project plan so to speak.
>
> This can really help you see exactly what steps you need to take next to move along that timeline, instead of just feeling like a deer in headlights.
>
> Time to create your timeline and obliterate the overwhelm!

CHAPTER 20

I'm Too Old or Too Young to Teach

I've heard both. When I started an education company at the age of 19, I can assure you I had crushing moments of self doubt and very open criticism and mocking from others about my age *'who on earth is going to listen to a 19 year old kid and even pay her to train their staff who are twice her age?!'*.

In short, it wasn't long before most of the critics asked me for a job when they saw the training contracts I had pouring through the door.

One of my course creation clients was 13 years old when she came to do her 'one day school set up session' with me. At that time she had 3 companies of her own. She didn't have years behind her, but by sitting down with me and really extrapolating what she had done to get to where she is, we identified that she had a string of strategies that she'd implemented for achieving what she has done.

We simply pulled together all of the steps she'd executed, applied a little curriculum design, and 10 hours later she had an online course teaching other young people how they can replicate her success.

I've also had people with years and years worth of experience have almost identical doubts that crosses the minds of the youngest edupreneurs *'Who would want to listen to me? I'm just an old fart compared to all these whizz kids out there?'*.

I'd say that 99.9% of the time, these feelings are all about self-esteem rather than age.

Being a good teacher has very little, if anything to do with age.

It's about learning how to best share your unique skills,

experiences and knowledge.

It's about imparting to others the shortcuts, tricks, systems, processes and methodologies that YOU have in the way YOU see, use, apply and contextualise them.

The world can be a better place because of you. All you have to do is start.

Time To Create Your Online Course!

Hopefully this book has addressed those fears, shut those self-doubts away forever, boshed those excuses out of the playing field and encouraged you to pull on those boots and get striving.

The only thing between where you are now and where you want to be, is yourself.

It's time to start, and I'm cheering you on all the way!

Don't forget to join my Facebook group for mutual support: 'Entrepreneur to Edupreneur - Course Creators'.

If you're ready to get moving there are a few ways that I can help you create your courses:

1. Attend the Course Creation Bootcamp: www.sarahcordiner.com/bootcamp

2. We 'do it for you': www.sarahcordiner.com/services

3. Book a one on one with me personally: www.sarahcordiner.com/services

4. DIY by taking my online courses on course creation: www.sarahcordiner.com/courses

Connect With Sarah

Let's get connected!
Here are all of the ways we can stay in touch:

Web: www.sarahcordiner.com
Web: www.maintraining.com.au

Podcast: www.coursecreatorspodcast.com

Sarah's Online Courses: www.sarahcordiner.com/course
Sarah's Amazon Books:
http://www.sarahcordiner.com/amazon
Youtube: http://www.sarahcordiner.com/youtube
LinkedIn: https://www.linkedin.com/in/sarahcordiner
Blog: www.sarahcordiner.com/blog
Slideshare:
http://www.slideshare.net/sarahcordiner/presentations
Twitter: https://twitter.com/CordinerSarah

Entrepreneur to EDUpreneur Facebook Group:
https://www.facebook.com/groups/entrepreneur2edupreneur/

Company Facebook: www.facebook.com/maintraining
Personal Facebook:
https://www.facebook.com/CordinerSarah

Company Web:
www.maintraining.com.au

Google+: www.google.com/+SarahCordinerEDU
Instagram: https://instagram.com/maintraining/

www.ingramcontent.com/pod-product-compliance
Lightning Source LLC
Chambersburg PA
CBHW070547170426
43201CB00012B/1748